INTRODUCTION

During World War I the submarine established itself as a major weapon of war, capable not only of inflicting severe damage to shipping, but also of totally altering the strategic situation. Consequently the major navies of the world set about developing their submarine fleets after the end of the war. Britain alone stood out against submarine warfare; having nearly suffered defeat from the German submarine campaign of 1915-18, His Majesty's Government had no wish to see the proliferation of the submarine. At the Washington Naval Conference of 1921 Britain hoped to achieve a ban on all forms of submarine warfare, but the attempt was unsuccessful. Many smaller navies began to acquire submarines as a relatively cheap and quickly built means of exercising naval power within their own spheres of influence.

Between the wars many types of submarine design were evolved, but abandoned when found to be unsatisfactory for various reasons. The major navies attempted to develop the large cruiser type, but its very size created disadvantages, lack of manouevrability and vulnerability. Another type tried by many navies, but dropped, was the aircraft-carrying submarine. Again the sheer size of the vessel and its vulnerability while assembling and launching the aircraft led to its abandonment, except by the Japanese.

By the outbreak of World War II each of the major navies had developed a submarine strategy which clearly affected submarine design within that navy. Germany alone had developed the military and strategic use of submarines in mercantile warfare to a high degree. Even Germany, however, had problems, and the Navy suffered from political interference which prevented submarine warfare from being developed to its fullest extent. Initially German submarines suffered greatly from torpedo failures, but the fault was soon diagnosed and remedied. A multiplicity of designs was developed during the war along with novel forms of propulsion and greatly improved weapons systems. Fortunately for the Allies conflicting priorities led to a curtailment in development and production of these new submarines and Germany was forced to continue operating obsolete designs. In the face of advancing anti-submarine (A/S) techniques this led to heavy losses.

Italy also built up a sizeable fleet of submarines, but initially concentrated on development of the cruiser-type. These were intended to help in extending her East African Empire, but when this collapsed the designs were found to be totally unsuitable for operations in the Mediterranean. Realising the need to protect and control Mediterranean waters the Italians embarked on a large programme of construction of smaller type submarines shortly before the war. Italy suffered, however, from lack of a well defined policy regarding submarine warfare. One sphere in which they did excell, was in the use of midget and 'human torpedo' types. Here, mainly due to the driving energy of a few individuals, spectacular operations were undertaken with great success.

Japan, with an eye to Pacific operations, also built up her submarine fleet between the wars. Like the Italians the Japanese High Command ignored the strategic influence of the submarine on mercantile warfare. Japanese plans for submarine operations involved the boats acting as scouts for the Combined Fleet and in building up packs for attacking enemy fleet units. Japanese submarines tended to ignore A/S techniques (their own being of a generally rather low standard) and they consequently suffered heavily at the hands of the competent US A/S escorts protecting Fleet units. As a final desperate measure large numbers of one-man suicide craft were produced, but they failed to alter the course of the war.

DATA

Classes have been ar[...]ical data has been so a[...] the development of a p[...]each individual country. T[...] the following broad cate[...] Midget 30+tons, C[...]800 tons, Oceangoing 80[...]Fleet 1,500 tons, Minelaying and transport.

The tabular data has been arranged in columns in the following order:

1. Class name; 2. Type; 3. Displacement (standard surfaced/submerged); 4. Dimensions Metric (length overall, beam, draught); 5. Dimensions Imperial (as metric); 6. Horsepower (surfaced/submerged)/Speed (knots) (surfaced/submerged); 7. Radius of action (nautical miles) (surfaced/submerged)/speed (knots) (surfaced/submerged); 8. Fuel (tons); 9. Diving limit (fathoms); 10. Guns (bore in mm (ins)); 11. Torpedo Tubes (diameter in mm (ins)); 12. Positioning of torpedo tubes; 13. Number of torpedoes and/or mines (M) carried; 14. Complement.*

The technical history is arranged as follows:

1. Name; 2. Pendant number (where applicable); 3. Builder (the legend for these is given below); 4. Month of first commissioning under country where listed; 5. Fate. Space precludes listing full details of war losses; various intermediate post-war transfers and changes have been likewise omitted for reasons of space.

*Note: In the German section two sets of figures are quoted in columns 6 and 7 where diesels, electric motors and Walter turbines are fitted.

LIST OF ABBREVIATIONS

Countries:

Ca	Canada
Fr	France
Ne	Netherlands
No	Norway
Sp	Spain
UK	United Kingdom
US	United States of America
USSR	Russia

Fate Details:

BU	Broken up/scrapped
Canc	Cancelled
CTL	Constructive Total Loss
Int	Interned
MC	Marine Casualty (lost from natural causes or sunk in error by friendly forces)
S	Scrapped
Sc	Scuttled
Str	Stricken and removed from active service for sale as scrap
Su	Surrendered
Trf	Transferred
Lost	Lost in action with enemy forces

The author would like to acknowledge the assistance given by the Finnish, Italian and Royal Thai Navies.

LIST OF BUILDERS

No.	Builder	Country
1.	A/B Crichton-Vulcan, Turku (Abo)	FINLAND
2.	A.G. Vulkan (Stettin)	GERMANY
3.	A.G. Weser (Bremen)	GERMANY
4.	At. & Ch. de La Loire (Nantes)	FRANCE
5.	Blohm & Voss (Hamburg)	GERMANY
6.	Bremer Vulkan (Vegesack)	GERMANY
7.	Brest Navy Yard	FRANCE
8.	Canadian Vickers (Montreal)	CANADA
9.	Cant. Nav. de Quarnaro (Fiume)	ITALY
10.	Cant. Nav. Franco Tosi (Taranto)	ITALY
11.	Cant. Nav. Triestino (Monfalcone)	ITALY
12.	Cant. Riuniti dell'Adriatico (Monfalcone)	ITALY
13.	Caproni (Milan)	ITALY
14.	Chatham Dockyard	UNITED KINGDOM
15.	Ch. Dubigeon (Nantes)	FRANCE
16.	Ch. Worms (Le Trait)	FRANCE
17.	Cherbourg Navy Yard	FRANCE
18.	Danziger Werft (Danzig)	GERMANY
19.	De Schelde (Flushing)	NETHERLANDS
20.	Deutsche Werft (Genoa)	ITALY (German control)
21.	Deutsche Werft (Hamburg)	GERMANY
22.	Deutsche Werft (Kiel)	GERMANY
23.	Deutsche Werft (Monfalcone)	ITALY (German control)
24.	Deutsche Werft (Nicolaev & Linz)	RUSSIA (German control)
25.	Deutsche Werft (Toulon)	FRANCE (German control)
26.	Deutsche Werke (Kiel)	GERMANY
27.	Flender Werft (Lubeck)	GERMANY
28.	Flensburger Schiffsbau (Flensburg)	GERMANY
29.	Galatz Navy Yard	ROMANIA
30.	Germania Werft (Kiel)	GERMANY
31.	Hietalhaden Laivatelakka (Helsinki)	FINLAND
32.	Horten Navy Yard	NORWAY
33.	Howaldtswerke (Kiel)	GERMANY
34.	Howaldtswerke (Hamburg)	GERMANY
35.	Kawasaki (Kobe)	JAPAN
36.	Kawasaki (Senshu)	JAPAN
37.	Klockner (Ulm)	GERMANY
38.	Kure Navy Yard	JAPAN
39.	Lorient Navy Yard	FRANCE
40.	Mitsubishi (Kobe)	JAPAN
41.	Mitsubishi (Nagasaki)	JAPAN
42.	Mitsui (Tamano)	JAPAN
43.	Neptun Werft (Rostock)	GERMANY
44.	Nordseewerke (Emden)	GERMANY
45.	Oder-Terni-Orlando (La Spezia)	ITALY
46.	Oderwerke (Stettin)	GERMANY
47.	Ourazaki	JAPAN
48.	Rotterdam Dry Dock Co. (Rotterdam)	NETHERLANDS
49.	Sasebo Navy Yard	JAPAN
50.	Schichau (Danzig)	GERMANY
51.	Schichau (Elbing)	GERMANY
52.	Schneider (Châlons-sur-Saône)	FRANCE
53.	Seebeckwerft (Bremerhaven)	GERMANY
54.	Simmering, Graz & Pauker (Vienna)	GERMANY
55.	Stulcken & Sohn (Hamburg)	GERMANY
56.	Toulon Navy Yard	FRANCE
57.	Vickers-Armstrong (Barrow)	UNITED KINGDOM
58.	Wilhemshaven Navy Yard	GERMANY
59.	Wilton-Fijenoord (Schiedam)	NETHERLANDS
60.	Yokosuka Navy Yard	JAPAN

FINLAND

German Design: SAUKKO

Under the terms of the Versailles Peace Treaty Germany was forbidden to possess submarines, and all facilities for their design and construction had to be destroyed. As a step towards re-creating a new submarine arm a number of German submarine designers and constructors who had kept in touch after the First World War, designed and provided technical know-how for the construction of a number of submarines for the Finnish Navy. The first of these was the small coastal submarine *Saukko*. She was built for operations in the Baltic against the Russian Navy and as such was provided with a minelaying capability.

German Design: IKU TURSO, VESIHIISI, VETEHINEN

While preparing the design for the *Saukko* the Germans also prepared a design for a sea-going submarine for the Finnish Navy. Three submarines were built to this design and like the *Saukko* they were fitted for mine-laying, the mines being supplied by the Germans. Being designed for use against Russian bases (never very far from the Finnish bases) radius of action was not of prime importance to this design and only 20 tons of oil fuel were carried (as opposed to the 67 tons carried by the German Type VIIa based on this design – see page 6).

The *Vesehiisi,* built to a German design. *Courtesy Finnish Navy*

German Design: VESIKKO

For their third design for the Finnish Navy the Germans produced a much improved version of the *Saukko*. This submarine, the *Vesikko*, was much larger than the *Saukko* and fitted with three 533mm torpedo tubes as opposed to the two 457mm of the *Saukko*. The design of the *Vesikko* served as a basis for the German Type IIA submarine (see page 5). During the war all Finnish submarines operated in conjunction with the German Navy. At the end of the war the submarines were all laid up. Under the Treaty of Paris, signed in February 1947, Finland was prohibited from possessing submarines and they were all subsequently scrapped, except *Vesikko* which in 1953 was handed over to the museum at Suomenlinna where she is retained as a national monument.

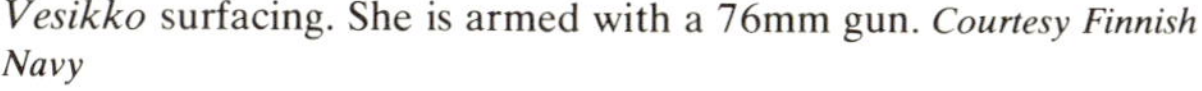

Vesikko surfacing. She is armed with a 76mm gun. *Courtesy Finnish Navy*

CLASS	*SAUKKO*	*VESIKKO*	*VETEHINEN*
TYPE	Coastal	Coastal	Seagoing
DISPLACEMENT	100/136	250/300	490/715
DIMENSIONS			
METRIC	32.5×4.12×3.2	40.9×3.96×4.12	63.5×6.1×3.05
IMPERIAL	106½×13½×10½	134×13×13½	208½×20×10
MACHINERY			
HP	200/150	700/360	1,060/600
SPEED	9/6	13/7	14/8
RADIUS	375/45	1,500/50	1,500/75
SPEED	8/4	10/4	10/4
FUEL		90	20
DIVING LIMIT		50	40
ARMAMENT			
GUNS	1×13	1×20	1×76 (3), 1mg
TORPEDO TUBES	2×457 (18)	3×533 (21)	4×533 (21)
SITING	2 bow	3 bow	2 bow, 2 stern
NO OF TORPEDOES/	2		6
MINES	+9M	+6M	+20M
COMPLEMENT	13	16	27

Name	Builder	In Service	Fate
Iku-Turso	1	1931	Str c1945
Saukko	31	1930	Str c1945
Vesihiisi	1	1930	Str c1945
Vesikko	1	1933	Museum 1953
Vetehinen	1	1930	Str c1945

GERMANY

Type IA: *U.25-26*

Following the abrogation of the Versailles Peace Treaty (which forbade the possession of submarines) Germany, in 1934, began to build up a new submarine fleet. Previous to this, and contrary to the terms of the peace treaty, Germany, had provided engineering assistance and technical know-how for the construction of submarines for the Finnish and Turkish Navies (see page 3). From these designs and certain of those developed during World War I (all of which were treated as prototypes) the German Naval Staff developed five basic submarine designs. The first of these was the seagoing Type IA based on the Turkish *Gür*. Two vessels of this type were completed and formed the basis for the succeeding seagoing type submarines, construction of which was given top priority at the start of the war.

Type IIA: *U.1-6* IIB*: *U.7-24, U.120-121* IIC†: *U.56-63* IID§: *U.137-152*

Parallel with the construction of seagoing submarines went that of the Type II coastal boats which were also given top priority. Design of this Type was based on the Finnish *Vesikko* (see page 4) and succeeding variants of this type were provided with increased bunkerage to extend the range. The Type IID were completed with saddle tanks which were partly used for the storage of oil fuel, almost doubling their range over the earlier boats. When used on war patrols provision was made for this type to mount two twin 20mm A/A guns. On the outbreak of war *U.120* and *U.121* were under construction for the Yugoslav Navy, but were requisitioned and commissioned into the German Navy. As the U-boat war moved away from the coasts of Britain this type was gradually relegated to training duties or transferred to the Black Sea.

Type II submarines. In the front row Type IIB and IID boats (*U.121* third from left) with Type IIB, IID and IIC boats behind (from left to right *U.60, U.6,* Type IID, *U.7, U.21*). *Author's Collection*

U.1. A Type IIA boat developed from the Finnish *Vesikko*. *Vicary*

U.23. Drüppel

Type III: Projected

An unusual design prepared in 1933, the Type III were to have been fitted with a circular hangar abaft the conning tower for the transport of two M.T.B.'s. Inherent disadvantages of the system, which required a calm sea for the submarine to flood down to enable the M.T.B.'s to be floated out of the hangar, led to the abandonment of the project. (In modified form similar ideas were adopted by the British, Italian and Japanese Navies during the war. qv.)

Type IV, V, VI: Projected (Details unknown)

Type VIIA: *U.27-36* VIIB*: *U.45-55, 73-76, 83-87, 99-102* VIIC†: *U.69-72, 77-82, 88-98, 132-136, 201-212, 221-232, 235-458, 465-486, 551-790, 821-840, 901-1058, 1063-1080* VIIC$^{41/42}$§: *U.1101-1220, 1271-1330* VIIC^{42}¶: *U.1093-1100, 1331-1404, 1417-1500, 1801-2110, 2301-2320* VIID: *U.213-218* VIIE: Projected (Details unknown) VIIF: *U.1059-1062*

This class was a smaller version of the Type I and based on the Finnish *Vetehinen* (see page 3). The Type VII were designed to be as small as possible, but still met the Staff requirements for a seagoing submarine. The design proved most successful and succeeding variants incorporated war experience with increased bunkerage and range so that the Type VIIC became the main operational submarine used by the Germans during the war. Although Allied advances in anti-submarine (A/S) techniques and the increasing power of the A/S escorts and aircraft rendered the Type VII obsolete by 1943-44 new advanced designs had not reached operational status. As a result they remained in service with heavily augmented A/A armament (see below) and many were fitted with the Schnorchel device.

The Type VIIE was to be powered by a new lightweight diesel engine which did not materialise. The Type VIIF was planned as a supply submarine, but never operated in this role for Allied air activity made replenishment at sea an almost impossible task.

U.428-430, 746-750 and *U.1161* were built for the Italian Navy to replace Italian submarines based at Bordeaux which were to be converted to transport vessels (see pages 37-38). When Italy surrendered in 1943 they were seized and incorporated back into the German Navy under their original numbers.

Typical A/A Modifications

Type	88mm (3.5in)	37mm	20mm
VIIB	removed	1	3 (3×1)
VIIC*	,,	1	4 (2×2)
VIIC$^{41/42}$	,,	removed in some	8 (2×2, 1×4)
VIIC^{42}	,,	2 or 4	6 (3×2)

(*U.441* experimentally fitted with one 37mm, and eight 20mm (2×4)

A pre-war view of *U-30* which sank the liner *Athenia* on September 3, 1939. *Drüppel*

The conning tower of *U.30* showing the 20mm A/A. *Author's Collection*

The conning tower of *U.46*. Note the buckled plating and bent periscope housing resulting from a depth charge attack. *Author's Collection*

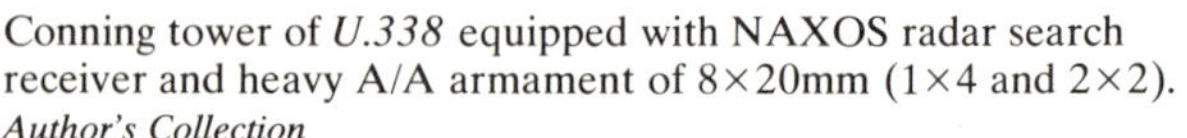

Conning tower of *U.338* equipped with NAXOS radar search receiver and heavy A/A armament of 8×20mm (1×4 and 2×2). *Author's Collection*

U.566 returning to harbour, the conning tower clearly showing damage suffered in a depth charge attack on November 17, 1942. *Author's Collection*

U.596 returning to harbour after a patrol. *U.596* was the first U-boat to be fitted with a schnorchel. *Author's Collection*

Type VIII: Projected (Details unknown)

Type IXA: *U.37-44* IXB*: *U.64-65, 103-111, 122-124* IXC†: *U.66-68, 125-131, 153-166, 171-176, 501-524, 841-846, 853-858, 865-870, 877-882, 889-894, 1221-1270, 1501-1530* IXC⁴⁰§: *U.167-170, 183-194, 525-550, 801-820* IXD¹: *U.180, 195* IXD²¶: *U.177-179, 181-182, 196-200, 847-852, 859-864, 871-876, 883-888, 895-900, 1531-1600*

Based on the *U.81* of World War I this oceangoing type was designed to undertake long range patrols in distant waters and therefore carried more torpedoes than the seagoing Type VII and also had greatly increased bunkerage.

A lack of certain essential raw materials for war production in Germany led to the development of the IXD, a transport submarine capable of carrying cargoes from the Far East. To increase capacity the torpedo tubes that were originally to have been fitted in the IXD¹ were omitted, and the battery capacity reduced. The Type IXD² was the military version of the transport model and was also designed for patrols in the Far East. Provision was made for eight vertical mine shafts to be fitted in place of the torpedo reloads, but this modification was rarely carried out.

In the late summer of 1942 *U.511*, while on service in the Baltic, conducted a series of experimental launchings of the Hecht missile (sometimes called the Do missile). A set of six launchers angled at 45° were welded to the deck of *U.511* abaft the conning tower. The launchings were carried out submerged from a depth of 40-feet near the rocket station at Peenemünde. The surface-to-surface rocket was 8-feet 2-inches long and had a range of 6 miles. Following the tests the launchers were removed from *U.511* and the idea dropped.

Typical A/A modifications

Type	105mm (4.1in)	37mm	20mm
IXA	1	1	2 (1×2)
IXB*	removed	removed	2 (2×1)
IXC	,,	1	4 (2×2)
IXC⁴⁰	,,	1	4 (2×2)
IXD²	,,	1	4 (2×2)

*Later eight 20mm (1×4, 2×2) then four 20mm (2×2) and one 37mm

U.805 surrendering off the American coast on May 15, 1945. Note the large number of A/A fitted. *Drüppel*

Left *U-123* and right *U.38* at Lorient in June 1941. *U.38* has just returned from patrol in the Freetown area where she sank eight ships of 47,279 grt. *Author's Collection*

Conning tower of *U.844*. Note the Hohentwiel radar aerial to starboard. *Drüppel*

Type XA: Projected (Details unknown) XB: *U.116-119, 219-220, 233-234*

The projected Type XA was a large oceangoing minelayer of about 2,500 tons. The mines were stored in vertical shafts in the saddle tanks and in vertical shafts in the after section of the hull. These latter projected above and below the pressure hull. The internal layout was considered to be wasteful of space and the overall design too large. The Type XA was therefore abandoned in favour of the much smaller Type XB.

The Type XB was able, as a result of its much improved design, to carry more mines than the Type XA and in addition was fitted with two stern torpedo tubes. The mines were housed in vertical shafts in the forward section of the hull which projected above and below the pressure hull, each shaft holding three mines. A further 24 mine shafts, each holding two mines, were sited to port and starboard in the saddle tanks. Although designed as minelayers these submarines were used more often as supply ships. Like other submarines these vessels had the deck gun removed and extra A/A armament in the form of two twin 20mm mounts replacing the single 20mm originally fitted.

U.116 entering Kiel some time in 1942. *Author's Collection*

Type XI: *U.112-115*

The Type XI was designed in 1938 as a cruiser-submarine capable of taking on a relatively heavily armed adversary in a surface engagement. The class was considered to be a much more practicable proposition than the Type III, being equipped with a small seaplane for scouting purposes. To carry out its surface role the Type XI was to have been fitted with very powerful diesels and would have been the fastest diesel-powered submarine afloat. Realising that submarine warfare had greatly altered since World War I and that this concept was no longer valid the project was abandoned before any of the vessels were laid down.

Type XII: Projected

The Type XII design was developed from the Type XI, the specification calling for a fleet type submarine with extended range and high surface speed. By the time the design had been completed Germany's surface fleet was acting as commerce raiders and there was no call for a fleet type submarine, so the project was abandoned.

Type XIII: Projected (Details unknown)

Limitations of armament and radius of action in the Type II coastal submarines led the German Staff to design the Type XIII of about 400 tons and 15 knots surfaced speed. Possibly designed for use in the constricted waters of the Mediterranean the Type XIII design was subsequently considered as unnecessary. The Type VII was more than adequate for use in the Mediterranean and the Type XIII would have been totally unsuitable for Atlantic operations. Furthermore the Type II was perfectly satisfactory for training purposes and thus there was no real need to divert shipyard capacity from top priority construction of the Type VII. The project was therefore abandoned.

Type XIV: *U.459-464, 487-500, 2201-2204*

Following experience with the Type IXD[1] supply submarines the Type XIV 'Broad-Beam' supply type with greatly increased cargo capacity was designed. The design was successful and proved the value of boats designed specifically for certain roles as opposed to those converted.

Type XV: Projected (Details unknown)

The need to extend the range of the Type VII submarines led the Germans to design a whole range of supply submarines, rather than develop a satisfactory long range, high endurance ocean-going submarine. The Type XV was yet another projected design for a supply submarine with workshop facilities for carrying out limited repairs at sea. The hull was formed of a triple cylinder of about 2,500 tons displacement. By the time the design was completed Allied air superiority and A/S attacks rendered surface replenishment by submarine an extremely hazardous procedure and the project was abandoned.

Type XVI: Projected (Details unknown)

This was another supply submarine similar to the Type XV but with displacement increased to 5,000 tons. As with the Type XV allied A/S techniques rendered the design impractical and the project was abandoned.

Experimental Boats: *VB.60, V.80, U.791* (ex-*V.300*)

These three experimental boats were all developed to test the ideas of Professor Helmuth Walter, who had designed a closed-cycle diesel and turbine engine. The first design, *VB.60*, although never built, provided valuable data from which larger boats using the closed-cycle turbine could be developed. The closed-cycle turbine was chosen as being the more valuable of the two systems for it was hoped that it would do away with alternative power supplies, with consequent savings in weight and space. *V.80* completed in 1940 was provided with an auxiliary electric motor. The hull design adopted the 'figure-of-eight' configuration which later became standard for all closed-cycle turbine-powered submarine. *V.300* was the sea-going prototype of the two previous designs, but it was found with *V.80* that a grave disadvantage of the Walter turbine was its very high fuel consumption at high speeds, which drastically reduced the radius of action. It was obvious that unless some improvement to fuel consumption could be made one of the major advantages of the novel propulsion system would be nullified. To obtain a suitable radius of action an auxiliary propulsion system would have to be fitted which would result in a greatly increased ratio of machinery weight to displacement and resultant loss of space available for armament and equipment. In view of the problems experienced *U.791* was never completed.

V.80 an experimental boat powered by a Walter turbine. *Drüppel*

Type XVIIA: *U.792-793, 794-795** XVIIB: *U.1405-1416* XVIIB$_2$†: Projected XVIIB$_3$††: Projected XVIIE: Projected XVIIG‡: *U.1081-1092* XVIIG$_2$¶: Projected XVIIK^0: *U.798-800*

The restricted radius of action of the Walter turbine made it a more practicable proposition for use in coastal submarines rather than the large oceangoing types. This led to the design of the Type XVII, but continued difficulties with the turbine led to the abandonment of most of the type, the XVIIE resorting to a conventional propulsion system with greatly increased battery capacity. The Type XVIIK relied on a closed-cycle diesel engine based on the Deschimag project of A.G. Weser (subsequently abandoned). To increase the radius of action the Type XVIIK was equipped with a large number of compressed air cylinders for the diesel. These took up so much space, however, that there was no room for reload torpedoes.

U.793, one of the first production boats to be powered by a closed-cycle Walter turbine. *Drüppel*

Type XVIII: *U.796-797*

The Type XVIII was the first ocean-going submarine designed to be powered by the Walter turbine. An auxiliary diesel/electric propulsion system had to be fitted owing to the restricted range of the turbine. The other problems with the turbine had still not been resolved, however, and construction was halted in 1944 pending improvements to the turbine. As these were not forthcoming construction of the Type XVIII was never resumed.

Type XIX: Projected (Details unknown)

With the abandonment of the Type XV and XVI supply submarines plans were prepared for a new supply boat of about 2,000 tons powered by a new disel. Work on the new engine ceased, however, and the project was abandoned in favour of the Type XX transport submarines.

Type XX: *U.1601-1800*

The Type XX transport submarines were designed on conventional lines following the failure of the new diesels for the Type XIX. This type was specifically designed for the transport of oil and raw materials from the Far East. During 1943, however, priority was given to the construction of the Type XXI and work on the Type XX was abandoned.

Type XXI: *U.2501-4000* XXIB*: Projected XXIC‡: Projected XXID$_1$: Projected supply XXID$_2$: Projected supply XXIE$_1$†: Projected supply XXIE$_2$†: Projected supply XXIT§: Projected supply XXIV§: Projected supply

The difficulties experienced with the Walter turbine led the Germans to prepare an alternative design for an oceangoing submarine with the emphasis placed on submerged performance. The design was streamlined and schnorchel-equipped and achieved more than double the underwater speed of the earlier schnorchel boats. Being designed to undertake continuously submerged patrols in any part of the world these boats were fully air-conditioned. The design made provision for the fitting of twin 30mm A/A guns but production difficulties with the mount led to the fitting of 20mm instead. Battery capacity was trebled and maximum underwater speed, which could only be maintained for about an hour, rose to 17¼ knots. For use under depth-charge attack the vessels were fitted with a silent electric motor coupled to each shaft. To speed construction the hull was fully welded and prefabricated in eight sections. Top priority was given to the construction of the Type XXI and work on all earlier Types ceased. A number of variations were made to the basic design, including supply versions. These modifications would have seriously delayed production of the basic design and they were abandoned. Even so Allied air raids on the canals and transport system in Germany delayed production badly and by the end of the war only two Type XXI had carried out an operational patrol.

U.2518. Drüppel

Type XXI submarines surrendered at Bergen. From left to right *U.3514, U.2511, U.2506. Author's Collection*

Type XXII: Projected

This type, developed from the Type XVII, was equipped with a single Walter turbine and carried an extra torpedo tube aft. Work on the design ceased at an early stage as it was felt it would be more profitable to press ahead with a design for a coastal version of the Type XXI.

Type XXIII: *U.2321-2500, 4500, 4701-5000*

The design for this coastal submarine was, like the Type XXI upon which it was based, fully welded in four pre-fabricated sections. Being designed for rapid quantity production these submarines were fitted with the barest minimum of equipment necessary, even the deck casing being omitted. Space was at a premium and torpedoes had to be loaded into the forward tubes by raising the bows clear of the water with a crane. In spite of the austerity of the design the seven vessels which carried out operational patrols before the end of the war fully proved the effectiveness of the design and were extremely difficult to detect with the apparatus the Allies had available at the time.

U.2332. Drüppel

U.2361. Author's Collection

Type XXIV: Projected

This was a design for another ocean-going submarine powered by the Walter turbine. Allied A/S superiority at this point in the war meant that normally a submarine could only expect to fire a single salvo of torpedoes at a target before it was either detected or more probably already under attack. This design aimed at having the maximum number of torpedoes ready for immediate use, the procedure being to fire as many as possible, using a mixture of acoustic and pattern-running torpedoes so that lining up for an attack was not such a lengthy procedure. After firing the submarine would move away from the area at maximum speed using the Walter turbine; there would be no time to reload and attack again in the same area. The original design planned for 18 tubes, but this was subsequently reduced to 12, six of the angled after tubes being removed. As before difficulties with the turbine and problems of manufacture or large submarines led to the abandoning of this project.

Type XXV: Projected

The possibility of an Allied landing somewhere in France led to the development of this submarine designed purely for coastal defence. As it was powered by a single electric motor the Staff subsequently felt that a midget submarine would be more suitable for the task envisaged, and the design was therefore abandoned.

Type XXVI: *U.4501-4700* XXVIA*: Projected XXVIB†: Projected XXVIE$_2$: Projected XXVIF§: Projected XXVIG‡: Projected

This design was a smaller seagoing submarine based on the Type XXIV. Only a single shaft was fitted, and to enable the batteries to be charged while schnorchelling an auxiliary diesel generator was fitted. Originally the design was for a vessel of 720/772 tons (176½×17½×18¼ ft—53.5×5.35×5.5m) but it was found that the hull would be unable to withstand the designed schnorchelling speed of 14½ knots from the 1,200 HP diesel. Consequently the hull was enlarged and a lower powered diesel fitted. Subsequent variations to the design (all of which were abandoned) increased the hull size still further to enable more powerful diesels to be fitted, increased battery capacity and reintroduced conventional diesel/electric propulsion.

Type 126W, 1260, 126K, 126E: Projected

These were all private venture designs powered by either Walter turbine, closed-cycle diesel or conventional diesel/electric with a high underwater speed. All the designs were abandoned.

Type XXVIIA (Hecht): *U.2111-2200, 2205-2300* XXVIIB*: *U.5001-6351*

Following the exploits of the Japanese, Italian and British midget submarines the Germans decided to embark on the construction of a similar type of vessel. The first design, Type XXVIIA (Hecht) was for a small 7-ton vessel armed with a limpet mine. They were powered by an electric motor and it was anticipated that the radius of action would be 90 miles. This was not, however, realised, for lack of a suitable small magnetic compass meant that the larger gyro equipment had to be fitted and for this the hull had to be enlarged resulting in a reduction in the radius of action. Finally a suitable mine was not forthcoming and the few craft completed to this design were used for training. The Type XXVIIB (Seehund) was developed from the Type XXVIIA and provision was made for the craft to carry two torpedoes slung underneath the hull. They were built primarily for coast-defence against the expected Allied invasion of Europe. Propulsion was provided by diesel/electric motors with optional additional external fuel tanks which greatly extended the radius of action.

Midget submarine of the Hecht type being prepared for operations. *Drüppel*

Seehund type midget. *Drüppel*

Type XXVIII: Projected

This was a design for yet another coastal submarine powered by the Walter turbine. Speed was sacrificed in order that a suitable radius of action could be obtained with the turbine, thus eliminating the necessity for fitting an auxiliary diesel engine.

Type XXIXA: Projected XXIXB*: Projected XXIXB2†: Projected XXIXC§: Projected XXIXD: Projected XXIXG††: Projected XXIXH‡: Projected XXIXK¼¶: Projected

This design of conventionally propelled seagoing boats successively increased in size through the various designs with increasing radius of action and armament. All were equipped with a silent electric motor for creeping. The final design was powered by a closed-cycle diesel engine.

Type XXX: Projected XXXA*: Projected XXXB†: Projected

This was a projected design for an oceangoing submarine similar to the Type XXI but with greatly increased battery capacity in the Type XXXA and XXXB. The design lacked any provision for a conning tower.

Type XXXI: Projected

Based on the Type XXXA this was another oceangoing design in which the requirement was for a greatly improved submerged performance. Propulsion and armament remained the same as the Type XXXA. The design was completed with a very low conning tower and the hull was short in comparison with other oceangoing Types.

Type XXXII: Projected

A midget design powered by very high-revving diesel engines similar to those fitted in MTB's. The diesels were closed-cycle. The torpedoes were slung underneath the hull in a similar way to those in the Seehund.

Type XXXIII: Projected

This was a design for a coastal submarine powered by a closed-cycle diesel engine. The oxygen for the diesel was stored in a large pressurised cylinder sited amidships within the pressure hull. To provide access to the forward part of the boat, a second small pressurised hull cylinder was positioned over the main pressure hull amidships; this also served as an attack centre.

Type XXXIV: Projected

This was a midget design developing a very high underwater speed from a closed-cycle fast-revving diesel engine. Oxygen for the engine was stored in a pressure cylinder in the fore part of the submarine. The submarine was armed with two torpedoes which were clamped to the outside of the pressure hull either side of the small conning tower.

Type XXXV: Projected

This design for a seagoing submarine was the last prepared which was to have been powered by the Walter turbine.

Type XXXVI: Projected (Details unknown)

Still anticipating problems with the Walter turbine an alternative design powered by four high-revving closed-cycle diesel engines was prepared in place of the Type XXXV. This was the last design prepared before the end of the war.

Neger

This was a one-man weapon which carried a standard torpedo slung underneath. Like all the succeeding midget-type craft these were developed specifically as anti-invasion weapons. They all suffered from a small radius of action, but being small craft were easily transportable by road and rail to areas of operation. About 200 of this type were built during 1944-45. Initial models had an open cockpit for the pilot, but this was later covered by a perspex dome. No breathing apparatus was provided and the weapon had to be steered towards its target on the surface, a distinct disadvantage.

Neger one-man torpedo. Note the perspex dome. *Drüppel*

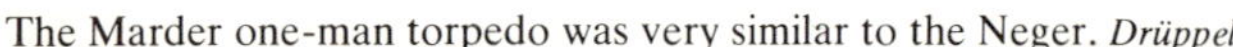

The Marder one-man torpedo was very similar to the Neger. *Drüppel*

Marder

This weapon was similar to the Neger but could be steered towards its target underwater. Like all the German small weapons they could only be used in fairly sheltered waters, which rather limited their capability against the Allied invasion forces off the Normandy coast and along the northern coast of Europe in general. Nearly 200 *Marders* were built between 1944-45.

Molch

This was a one-man weapon similar to the *Biber*, of which about 400 were built.

Biber

This one-man midget was probably the most successful of the small craft produced by the Germans. It was very similar in appearance to the British Welman type. Over 300 *Bibers* were built between 1944-45.

Hai

Only one prototype model was built of this one-man torpedo.

Delphin

Like the *Hai* this two-man torpedo was purely experimental and only two craft were built.

Biber, one of the most successful of the German midget types.
Author's Collection

Delphin. *Drüppel*

Molch. *Drüppel*

'K' Type

This was a projected midget submarine with a crew of two which would have been similar to the Type XVIIB.

FOREIGN SUBMARINES

Ex-Turkish: *UA* (ex-*BATIRAY*)
Ex-British *Porpoise* Class: *UB* (ex-*Seal*)
Ex-Norwegian: *'B'* Class: *UC.1* (ex-*B.5*), *UC.2* (ex-*B.6*)
Ex-Netherlands *'H'* Class: *UD.1* (ex-*0.8*) *0.12* Class: *UD.2* (ex-*0.12*) *0.21* Class: *UD.3-5* (ex-*0.25-27*)
Ex-French *L'Aurore* Class: *UF.1* (ex-*L'AFRICAINE*), *UF.2* (ex-*LA FAVORITE*), *UF.3* (ex-*L'ASTRÉE*), *UF.?* (ex-*L'ANDROMÉDE*)
Ex-Italian *'R'* Class: *UIT.1-3* (ex-*R.10-12*), *UIT.4-6* (ex-*R.7-9*)
Ex-Italian *Flutto* Class: *UIT.7* (ex-*BARIO*), *UIT.8* (ex-*LITIO*), *UIT.9* (ex-*SODIO*), *UIT.10* (ex-*POTASSIO*), *UIT.11* (ex-*RAME*), *UIT.12* (ex-*FERRO*), *UIT.13* (ex-*PIOMBO*), *UIT.14* (ex-*ZINCO*), *UIT.15* (ex-*SPARIDE*), *UIT.16* (ex-*MURENA*), *UIT.19* (ex-*NAUTILO*), *UIT.20* (ex-*GRONGO*)
Ex-Italian *'CM'* Class: *UIT.17-18* (ex-*CM.1-2*)
Ex-Italian *Calvi* Class: *UIT.21* (ex-*GIUSEPPE FINZI*)
Ex-Italian *Liuzzi* Class: *UIT.22* (ex-*ALPINO BAGNOLINI*), *UIT.23* (ex-*REGINALDO GIULIANI*)
Ex-Italian *Cappelini* Class: *UIT.24* (ex-*COMANDANTE CAPPELINI*)
Ex-Italian *Marconi* Class: *UIT.25* (ex-*LUIGI TORELLI*)

UA, taken over by Germany while under construction for Turkey as the *Batiray*. *Drüppel*

CLASS	*VB.60*	*V.80*	*U.791*	Deschmag	126W
TYPE	Experimental	Experimental	Experimental	Experimental	Experimental
DISPLACEMENT	60	73¼/76	610/655	352	863
DIMENSIONS					
METRIC	21×1.9	22×2.1×3.2	52×4.2×5.5	35.5×4.2×4.2	50×5.1×6.4
IMPERIAL	68¾×6½	72¼×7×10½	171×13¼×18	118×13¼×13¾	163½×16½×21
MACHINERY					
HP	2,000	2,000 + 14	4,360 + 300/150	3,000 + 50	7,500 + 580 + 265/536 + 71
SPEED		28 4	19 9¼/9½	15¾/22¾ 4	23 4
RADIUS		50	205 + 2,330/40		240
SPEED		28	19 9/9½		20
FUEL		20 Perhydrol	98 (Perhydrol) 34 (Oil)	9½ (Oxygen) 30 (Oil)	120 (Perhydrol) 115 (Oil)
DIVING LIMIT					
ARMAMENT					
GUNS	—	—	—	—	
TORPEDO TUBES	—	—	2×533 (21)	2×533 (21)	8×533 (21)
SITING	—	—	2 bow	2 bow	8 bow
NO OF TORPEDOES/	—	—	6	4	10
COMPLEMENT	3	4	25		

CLASS	*1260*	*126K*	*126E*
TYPE	Experimental	Experimental	Experimental
DISPLACEMENT	870	864	894
DIMENSIONS			
METRIC	50×5.4×6.4	47.2×5.2×6.4	50×6×6.4
IMPERIAL	163×17¾×21	155¾×17×21	164×19¾×21
MACHINERY			
UNIT	7,500 + 580 + 265/536 + 71	4,500 + 200	3,600/4,000 + 200
SPEED	23 4	20 6	20 6
RADIUS	140	160	27
SPEED	20	20	20
FUEL	40 (Oxygen) 110(Oil)	40 (Oxygen) 100 (Oil)	90 (Oil)
DIVING LIMIT			
ARMAMENT			
GUNS	—	—	
TORPEDO TUBES	8×533 (21)	8×533 (21)	8×533 (21)
SITING	8 bow	8 bow	8 bow
NO OF TORPEDOES/ MINES	10	10	10
COMPLEMENT			

CLASS	*XXVII*	*XXXII*	*XXXIV*	*NEGER/MARDER*	*BIBER*	*MOLCH*
TYPE	Midget	Midget	Midget	Midget	Midget	Midget
DISPLACEMENT	11¾ (15*)	90	90	5	6¼	10¾
DIMENSIONS						
METRIC	10(12*)×1.3(1.7*)×1.4		23.4×2.48×2.5	8.07×3.28×1.07	9×1.6×1.4	10.85×1.8×1.8
IMPERIAL	34(39*)×4¼(5½*)×4½		78×8¼×8½	26¼×1¾×3½	29½×5¼×4¾	35½×6×6
MACHINERY						
HP	12(60/11*)	1,500	1,500 + 35	12	32/13	13
SPEED	5¾(7¾*)/6	22	10/22 6	20	6½/5¼	4¼/5
RADIUS	40(70 with extra battery) (300/60*)	200	1,200/90	30	125/10	50/40
SPEED	4 (7/3)	12	11/22	3	6/5	4/5
FUEL	½ (in * only)	6 (Oxygen)	6½ (Oxygen) 5¼ (Oil)	—		
DIVING LIMIT						
ARMAMENT						
GUNS	—	—	—	—	—	—
TORPEDO TUBES	—	—	—	—	—	
SITING	—	—	—	—	—	—
NO OF TORPEDOES/ MINES	1M or T (2T*)	2	2	1	2	2
COMPLEMENT	2		3	1	1	1

CLASS	*HAI*	*DELPHIN*	*'K'*
TYPE	Midget	Midget	Midget
DISPLACEMENT	5	5	c18
DIMENSIONS			
METRIC	8.07×.32×.32		11.6×1.9×1.3
IMPERIAL	26¼×1¾×1¾		38×6¼×4½
MACHINERY			
HP	12	12	95/25
SPEED	20	20	9/6
RADIUS	30		
SPEED	3		
FUEL			
DIVING LIMIT			
ARMAMENT			
GUNS	—	—	—
TORPEDO TUBES	—	—	—
SITING	—	—	—
NO OF TORPEDOES/ MINES	1		2
COMPLEMENT	1	2	2

CLASS	*II*	*XVIIA*	*XVIIB*
TYPE	Coastal	Coastal	Coastal
DISPLACEMENT	254/303(279/329*, 291/341†, 314/364§)	313(236*)/343(259*)	312(306†, ††)/337
DIMENSIONS			
METRIC	40.9(42.7*,44†§)×4.1(4.9§)×3.8(3.9*§)	38(34.1*)×?(3.4*)×?(4.6*)	41.5(40.7†, ††)×4.5×4.3(4.9†, ††)
IMPERIAL	134¼(140*,144†§)× 13½(16§)×12½(12¾*§)	124¾(111¼*)×?(11¼*)×?(15*)	136¼(133†,††)×14¾×14(16†, ††)

CLASS	*II*	*XVIIA*	*XVIIB*
MACHINERY			
HP	700/360(410†§)	5,000(2,500 in U793) + 210/77	2,500(1,160†) + 210(not in ††)/77
SPEED	13(12†, 12¾§)/7(7¼§)	26(21 in U793) + 9/5	21½(15¾†, 20††) + 8½(9†)/5
RADIUS	1,050(1,800*, 1,900†, 3,500§)/35(43*†, 56§)	80 + 1,840/76(40*)	150(660†, 1,700††) + 3000/40
SPEED	12(21*, 23†, 38§) 12/4	26 + 9/2(4½*)	20(15¾†, 8††) + 8/4½
FUEL		40 (Aurol) (Perhydrol*) 17 (14*) (Oil)	55 (Aurol)(100 Perhydrol†, 80 Perhydrol††) 20 (Oil) not in ††
DIVING LIMIT	80		
ARMAMENT			
GUNS	1×20	—	—
TORPEDO TUBES	3×533 (21)	2×533 (21)	2×533 (21)
SITING	3 bow	2 bow	2 bow
NO OF TORPEDOES/ MINES	5 or 18M	4	4 (2†, ††)
COMPLEMENT	25	12	19

CLASS	*XVIIE*	*XXII*	*XXIII*	*XXV*
TYPE	Coastal	Coastal	Coastal	Coastal
DISPLACEMENT	340(314‡, 320¶, 368°)/345	155/200	234/258	160
DIMENSIONS				
METRIC	44(39.6‡, 43¶, 40.7°)×3.28(3.4‡°, 3.58¶)×4.3(4.7‡, 4.4¶, 4.8°)	27.2×2.98×3.9	34.6×2.98×3.7	28×2.98
IMPERIAL	144(129¾‡, 141¾¶, 133½°)×10¾(11¼‡°, 11¾¶)×14(15½‡, 14½¶, 16°)	89×9¾×12¾	113¾×9¾×12¼	92×9¾
HP	900(210‡¶, 1,500°)/1,160(77‡¶°)[1] + 2,500	1,750 + 210/77	575/600 + 35	160
SPEED	11½(8½‡¶, 14°)/14½(5‡¶°) + 25	20 + 7/7	9¾/12½ + 4½	9
RADIUS	6,000(3,000‡¶, 1,600°)/224(40‡¶, 45°) + 114[2]	100 + 1,550/40	1,350/175	400
SPEED	8(12°)/4(4½‡¶°) + 20	20 + 6/4½	9¾/4	6
FUEL	40(20‡¶ 3°) (oil), 55 (Aurol in ‡, ¶ only)	30 (Aurol) 12 (Oil)	18	—
DIVING LIMIT				
ARMAMENT				
GUNS—	—	—	—	
TORPEDO TUBES	2×533 (21)	2×533 (21)	2×533 (21)	2×533 (21)
SITING	2 bow	2 bow	2 bow	2 bow
NO OF TORPEDOES/ MINES	4 (2°)	2	2	2
COMPLEMENT	19	12	14	

[1] Type XVIIK 16kts Schnorchelling
[2] Type XVIIK 120 @ 6 on closed-cycle

CLASS	*XXVIII*	*XXXIII*
TYPE	Coastal	Coastal
DISPLACEMENT	200	360
DIMENSIONS		
METRIC	32×	40×4×4
IMPERIAL	105×	131¼×13¼×13¾
MACHINERY		
HP	250 + 35	580 + 50
SPEED	8/10 + 5	9½/11½ + 5
RADIUS	2,000/250	4,500/1,600
SPEED	6/5	8/6
FUEL	(Durol)	25½ (Oxygen) 23½ (Oil)

CLASS	*XXVIII*	*XXXIII*
DIVING LIMIT		
ARMAMENT		
GUNS	—	—
TORPEDO TUBES	4×533 (21)	4×533(21)
SITING	4 bow	4 bow
NO OF TORPEDOES/ MINES	4	6
COMPLEMENT		

CLASS	*I*	*VII*	*XXVI*
TYPE	Seagoing	Seagoing	Seagoing
DISPLACEMENT	862/983	626(753*,769†§,999¶)/745(857*,871†§,1,050¶)	842(950*,1,150†)/926
DIMENSIONS			
METRIC	72.4×6.2×4.3	64.5(66.5*,67†§,68.5¶)×5.9(6.2*†§,6.8¶)×4.4(4.7*,4.8†§,5¶)	56.2(58.5*,62†)×5.5(6.4*†) ×5.95(6.4*)
IMPERIAL	237½×20¼×14	211¾(218¼*,220¼†§,225½¶)×19¼(20¼*†§,22¼¶) ×14½(15½*,15¾†§,16½¶)	184½(190¼*,203½†)×18(21*†) ×19½(21¼*)
MACHINERY			
HP	2,800/1,000	2,300(2,800*†§,2,700¶)/750	7,500
SPEED	17¾/8¼	16(17*†§,16¾¶)/8(7½†§¶)	24(22½*,21¼†) +
HP			580(2,000*†)+265/580
SPEED			11(15½*15†)/10(12*,11†) +
HP			70
SPEED			5
RADIUS	6,700/90	4,300(6,500*†§,10,000¶)/95(90*,80†§¶)	160 + 7,300/100 (Figures for * and †
SPEED	12/4	12/4	24 10/4 unknown
FUEL	96	67(108*, 114†§, 180¶)	97 (Perhydrol) (*unknown, 130 (Aurol) in †) 65 (Oil) (*unknown)
DIVING LIMIT	60	60 (74†§¶)	
ARMAMENT			
GUNS	1×105 (4.1) 1×20	1×88 (3.5) 1×20(2 in †§¶), 1×37(in †§¶ only)	4×30(2×2) (Not in XXVI)
TORPEDO TUBES	6×533 (21)	5×533 (21)	10×533 (21) (12*†)
SITING	4 bow 2 stern	4 bow 1 stern	4 bow 6 broadside (6 bow*†)
NO OF TORPEDOES/ MINES	14 or 42M	11 or 33(39*§¶)M (12 or 14M in *, 14T or 14M in †§¶)	10 (12*†)
COMPLEMENT	43	44 (45¶)	35 (*† unknown)

CLASS	*XXVIE*$_2$	*XXIXA*
TYPE	Seagoing	Seagoing
DISPLACEMENT	830(880§,800‡)	681(753*,790†,825§)
DIMENSIONS		
METRIC	55(57‡,53‡)×5.5(5.4§)×6.4	53.7(57.5*,57†,61.5§)×4.8×5.1(6†)
IMPERIAL	180½(187§,174‡)×18(17¾§)×21	176¼(188¾*,187†,201§)×15¾×16¾(19¾†)
MACHINERY		
HP	1,400+265(1,500§,750+265‡)/2,400(1,800§,2,800‡)	750+265(1,500+265†)/1,400(2,100*,2,400†,2,800§)
SPEED	14½(13½§,12‡)/16(15½§,16½‡) +	12(15¼†,11¾§)/13¾(15½*,16½†,16¾§) +
HP	120	70(110*,120†,140§)
SPEED	5	5
RADIUS	8,500(6,500§,8,400‡)/400	7,100/125(175*,235†,250§)
SPEED	10/6	10/6
FUEL		
DIVING LIMIT		
ARMAMENT		
GUNS	—	—
TORPEDO TUBES	8×533 (21)	8×533 (21)
SITING	4 bow, 4 broadside fwd (6 bow, 2 broadside fwd ‡)	8 bow
NO OF TORPEDOES/MINES		
COMPLEMENT	31	

CLASS	*XXIXD*	*XXXV*
TYPE	Seagoing	Seagoing
DISPLACEMENT	1,035(1,122††,715‡)	850
DIMENSIONS		
METRIC	67(58††,52‡)×5.4(6.7††,6.4‡)×5.35(6††,4.6‡)	50
IMPERIAL	218¾(189¾††,170½‡)×17¾(22††,21‡)×17½(19¾††,15‡)	164× ×
MACHINERY		
HP	1,200+265(750+750††,580+580‡)/2,100(2,800††,1,400‡)	7,500
SPEED	15(12††,13‡)/14¾(16½††,15½‡)	22
	+	+
HP	110(140††)1,500+580/375¶)	2,000/175
SPEED	5	+
RADIUS	7,100(10,000††,9,000‡)/150(225††,120‡)	160
SPEED	10/6	22
FUEL		40 (Aurol) 25 (Oxygen)
DIVING LIMIT		
ARMAMENT		
GUNS	—	—
TORPEDO TUBES	12×533 (21) (10††,6‡)	8×533 (21)
SITING	8 bow, 6 broadside fwd (6 bow, 4 broadside fwd ††, 6‡)	8 bow
NO OF TORPEDOES/ MINES	12	12
COMPLEMENT		

CLASS	*IX*	*XVIII*	*XXI*
TYPE	Oceangoing	Oceangoing	Oceangoing
DISPLACEMENT	1,032(1,051*,1,120†,1,144§,1,616¶) /1,153(1,178*,1,232†,1,247§,1,804¶)	1,485/1,652	1,621/1,819 (‡ unknown)
DIMENSIONS			
METRIC	76.5(76.4†,76.8§,87.6¶)×6.5(6.8*†,6.9§,7.5¶)×4.7(5.4¶)	71.5×6.1×6.4	76.7(83‡)×8×6.3(6.1*‡)
IMPERIAL	251(252†,251§,287½¶)× 21¼(22¼*†,22¾§,24½¶)×15½(17¾¶)	235¼×20¼×21	251¾(272¼‡)×21¾×20¾(20¼*‡)
MACHINERY			
HP	4.400(5,400¶)/1,000(1,100¶)	15,000 + 2,000/396	4,000/5,000(4,200*‡) + 226(220*‡)
SPEED	18(18½*,19¼¶)/7¾(7¼*†§,7¶)	24 18¼/7	15½/17¼(15½*‡) 6(5*‡)
RADIUS	8,100(8,700*,11,000†,11,400§,23,700¶)/78(64*,63†§,57¶)	200 + 5,200/40	11,150/285 (*‡ unknown)
SPEED	12/4	24 12/4½	12/6
FUEL	154(166*,208†,214§,442¶)	204 (Aurol) 124 (Oil)	234 (*‡ unknown)
DIVING LIMIT	60		74
ARMAMENT			
GUNS	1×105 (4.1) 1×37 1×20	4×30 (2×2)	4×30 (2×2)
TORPEDO TUBES	6×533 (21)	6×533 (21)	6×533 (21) (12*, 18‡)
SITING	4 bow 2 stern	6 bow	6 bow (+6 broadside*, 12 broadside‡)
NO OF TORPEDOES/ MINES	22 or 6+42M (not in †) or 66M 24 or 6+32M (in ¶ only) or 72M	23	20 or 14+18 small M or 12 large M (12*,18‡)
COMPLEMENT	48 (49§, 57¶)	52	58

CLASS	*XXIV*	*XXX*	*XXXI*
TYPE	Oceangoing	Oceangoing	Oceangoing
DISPLACEMENT	1,800	1,180 (1,170†)	1,200

CLASS	*XXIV*	*XXX*	*XXXI*
DIMENSIONS			
METRIC	71.5×6.1×6.5	69(65.5†)×5.4×6.1	54×6.1×7
IMPERIAL	234½×20¼×21¾	226(215½†)×17¾×20¼	177¼×20¼×23
MACHINERY			
HP	15,000 + 4,000/550 + 226	2,000/2,800 + 113(140*†)	2,000/2,800
SPEED	22 15/7 5	12(14½*†)/14½(15½*15¾†) 2(5*†)	14½/16½
RADIUS		15,000(15,500*†)/210	15,500/245
SPEED		10/6	10/6
FUEL	(Perhydrol)		
DIVING LIMIT			
ARMAMENT			
GUNS	4×30 (2×2)	—	—
TORPEDO TUBES	12×533 (21)	12×533 (21)* 8×533 (21)†	12×533 (21)
SITING	6 bow, 6 aft	8 bow, 4 broadside fwd* 8 bow‡	8 bow, 4 broadside fwd
NO OF TORPEDOES/ MINES	14	12*	
COMPLEMENT			

CLASS	*XII*	*III*	*XI*	*VIID*	*XB*
TYPE	Fleet	Cruiser	Cruiser	Minelayer	Minelayer
DISPLACEMENT	c1,600		3,140/3,630	965/1,080	1,763/2,177
DIMENSIONS					
METRIC		79×8×5.2	115×9.5×6.1	76.9×6.4×5	89.8×9.2×4.7
IMPERIAL		254¼×26¼×17	377¼×31¼×20¼	252¼×21×16½	294¾×30¼×13½
MACHINERY					
HP	7,000/1,680	2,800/1,000	17,600/2,200	2,800/750	4,800/1,100
SPEED	22/10	17/8	23/7	16/7¼	17/7
RADIUS	20,000/			8,100/69	14,550/95
SPEED	12/			12/4	12/4
FUEL				170	368
DIVING LIMIT				60	60
ARMAMENT					
GUNS		1×105 (4.1)	4×127 (5)(2×2) 2×37(2×1), 2×20 (1×	1×37 2×20 (2×1)	1×105 (4.1) 1×37, 1×20
TORPEDO TUBES	8×533 (21)	6×533 (21)	8×533 (21)	5×533 (21)	2×533 (21)
SITING	6 bow 2 stern	4 bow 2 stern	6 bow 2 stern	4 bow 1 stern	2 stern
NO OF TORPEDOES/ MINES		8 + 2 MTB's	12 + 1 aircraft	12+15M or 39M	15+22M or 66M
COMPLEMENT		65	110	44	52

CLASS	*VIIF*	*IXD*	*XIV*	*XX*	*XXID*
TYPE	Supply/Transport	Supply/Transport	Supply/Transport	Transport	Supply/Transport
DISPLACEMENT	1,084/1,181	1,610/1,799	1,688/1,932	2,708/2,962	1,949(2,809†, § ?)
DIMENSIONS					
METRIC	76.9×7.3×5	87.6×7.5×5.4	67.1×9.4×6.5	77×9.2×6.6	76.5(78†)×6.55×6.1
IMPERIAL	254¾×24×16	287½×24½×17¾	220¼×30¾ ×21¼	255×30¼ ×21¾	251¾(256†)×21¾×20¼

CLASS	*VIIF*	*IXD*	*XIV*	*XX*	*XXID*
MACHINERY					
HP	2,800/750	2,800/1,100	2,800/750	2,800/940	4,000/4,200 220 (not†)
SPEED	17/8	17/7	15/6½	12½/6	15½(10½†,15¼§)/16(14†,15½§) ‡ 5
RADIUS	9,500/75	9,900/115	9,300/55	13,000/50	11,300(20,000†,§ unknown)/155(110†, §?)
SPEED	12/4	12/4	12/4	12/4	10(4†)/6(4†)
FUEL	199	203	203	470	
DIVING LIMIT	60	60	60	60	
ARMAMENT					
GUNS	1×37 2×20	1×37 4×20 (2×2)	2×37 (2×1) 1×20	1×37 4×20 (2×2)	
TORPEDO TUBES	5×533 (21)	—	—	—	2×533 (21) (only in D², E², T and V)
SITING	4 bow 1 stern	—	—	—	2 bow
NO OF TORPEDOES/ MINES	14+25T as cargo	252 Tons of oil fuel as cargo	4 as cargo+ 432 Tons oil as cargo	700 Tons of oil fuel as cargo	2+430 Tons oil fuel as cargo (800 Tons d.w. in † and 275 tons d.w. in §)
COMPLEMENT	46	57	53	58	

Name	Builder	In Service	Fate
U.1	26	6/35	Lost 16/4/40
U.2	26	7/35	MC 8/4/44
U.3	26	8/35	Surr 5/45. Str
U.4	26	8/35	Surr 5/45. Str
U.5	26	8/35	MC 19/3/43
U.6	26	9/35	Su 5/45. Str
U.7	30	7/35	MC 18/2/44
U.8	30	8/35	Sc 5/45
U.9	30	8/35	Lost 20/8/44
U.10	30	9/35	Surr 5/45. Str
U.11	30	9/35	Surr 5/45. Str
U.12	30	9/35	Lost 8/10/39
U.13	26	11/35	Lost 31/5/40
U.14	26	1/36	Sc 5/45
U.15	26	3/36	MC 1/2/40
U.16	22	5/36	Lost 24/10/39
U.17	26	12/35	Sc 5/45
U.18	26	1/36	Sc 9/44
U.19	26	1/36	Sc 9/44
U.20	26	2/36	Sc 9/44
U.21	26	8/36	S 2/45
U.22	26	8/36	Lost 25/4/40
U.23	26	9/36	Sc 9/44
U.24	26	10/36	Sc 9/44
U.25	3	4/36	Lost 3/8/40
U.26	3	5/36	Lost 3/7/40
U.27	3	8/36	Lost 20/9/39
U.28	3	9/36	MC 3/44
U.29	3	11/36	Sc 5/45
U.30	3	10/36	Sc 5/45
U.31	3	12/36	Lost 2/11/40
U.32	3	4/37	Lost 30/10/40
U.33	30	7/36	Lost 12/2/40
U.34	30	9/36	MC 5/8/43
U.35	30	11/36	Lost 29/11/39
U.36	30	12/36	Lost 4/12/39
U.37	3	8/38	Sc 5/45
U.38	3	10/38	Sc 5/45
U.39	3	12/38	Lost 14/9/39
U.40	3	2/39	Lost 13/10/39
U.41	3	4/39	Lost 5/2/40
U.42	3	7/39	Lost 13/10/39
U.43	3	8/39	Lost 30/7/43
U.44	3	11/39	Lost 20/3/40
U.45	30	6/38	Lost 16/10/39
U.46	30	11/38	Sc 5/45
U.47	30	12/38	Lost 7/3/41
U.48	30	4/39	Sc 5/45
U.49	30	8/39	Lost 15/4/40
U.50	30	12/39	Lost 29/4/40
U.51	30	8/38	Lost 20/8/40
U.52	30	2/39	Sc 5/45
U.53	30	6/39	Lost 21/2/40
U.54	30	9/39	Lost 12/4/40
U.55	30	11/39	Lost 30/1/40
U.56	26	11/38	Lost 28/4/45
U.57	26	12/38	MC 3/9/40
U.58	26	2/39	Sc 5/45
U.59	26	3/39	Surr 5/45 BU
U.60	26	7/39	Sc 5/45
U.61	26	8/39	Sc 5/45
U.62	26	12/39	Sc 5/45
U.63	26	1/40	Lost 25/2/40
U.64	3	12/39	Lost 13/4/40
U.65	3	2/40	Lost 28/4/41
U.66	3	3/40	Lost 6/5/44
U.67	3	5/40	Lost 16/7/43
U.68	3	6/40	Lost 10/4/44
U.69	30	4/40	Lost 17/2/43
U.70	30	3/40	Lost 8/3/41
U.71	30	5/40	Sc 5/45
U.72	30	4/40	Lost 30/3/45
U.73	6	9/40	Lost 16/12/43
U.74	6	10/40	Lost 2/5/42
U.75	6	12/40	Lost 28/12/41
U.76	6	12/40	Lost 5/4/41
U.77	6	1/41	Lost 28/3/43
U.78	6	2/41	Lost 16/4/45
U.79	6	3/41	Lost 23/12/41
U.80	6	4/41	MC 28/11/44
U.81	6	4/41	Lost 9/1/44
U.82	6	5/41	Lost 6/2/42
U.83	27	2/41	Lost 4/3/43
U.84	27	4/41	Lost 24/8/43
U.85	27	6/41	Lost 14/4/42
U.86	27	7/41	Lost 29/11/43
U.87	27	8/41	Lost 4/3/43
U.88	27	10/41	Lost 14/9/42
U.89	27	11/41	Lost 14/5/43
U.90	27	12/41	Lost 24/7/42
U.91	27	1/42	Lost 25/2/44
U.92	27	3/42	Lost 4/10/44
U.93	30	7/40	Lost 15/1/42
U.94	30	8/40	Lost 28/8/42
U.95	30	8/40	Lost 28/11/41
U.96	30	9/40	Lost 30/3/45
U.97	30	9/40	Lost 16/6/43
U.98	30	10/40	Lost 19/11/42
U.99	30	11/40	Lost 17/3/41
U.100	30	11/40	Lost 17/3/41
U.101	30	12/40	Surr 5/45 BU
U.102	30	1/41	Lost 30/6/40
U.103	3	7/40	Lost 15/4/45
U.104	3	8/40	Lost 21/11/40
U.105	3	9/40	Lost 2/6/43
U.106	3	9/40	Lost 2/8/43
U.107	3	10/40	Lost 18/8/44
U.108	3	10/40	Lost 11/4/44
U.109	3	12/40	Lost 4/5/43
U.110	3	11/40	Lost 9/5/41
U.111	3	12/40	Lost 4/10/41
U.112-U.115	3	—	Projected
U.116	30	7/41	Lost 20/10/44
U.117	30	10/41	Lost 7/8/43
U.118	30	12/41	Lost 12/6/43
U.119	30	4/42	Lost 24/6/43
U.120	27	4/40	Sc 5/45
U.121	27	5/40	Sc 5/45
U.122	3	3/40	Lost 21/6/40
U.123	13	5/40	Surr 5/45. Fr *Blaison*, Str 1957
U.124	3	6/40	Lost 2/4/43
U.125	3	3/41	Lost 6/5/43
U.126	3	3/41	Lost 3/7/43
U.127	3	4/41	Lost 15/12/41
U.128	3	5/41	Lost 17/5/43
U.129	3	5/41	Sc 8/44
U.130	3	6/41	Lost 12/3/43
U.131	3	7/41	Lost 17/12/41
U.132	6	5/41	MC 5/11/42
U.133	6	7/41	Lost 14/3/42
U.134	6	7/41	Lost 24/8/43
U.135	6	8/41	Lost 15/7/43
U.136	6	8/41	Lost 11/7/42
U.137	26	6/40	Sc 5/45
U.138	26	6/40	Lost 18/6/41
U.139	26	7/40	Sc 5/45

Name	Builder	In Service	Fate
U.140	26	8/40	Sc 5/45
U.141	26	8/40	Sc 5/45
U.142	26	9/40	Sc 5/45
U.143	26	9/40	Surr 5/45†
U.144	26	10/40	Lost 9/8/41
U.145	26	10/40	Su 5/45 †
U.146	26	10/40	Sc 5/45
U.147	26	12/40	Lost 2/6/41
U.148	26	12/40	Sc 5/45
U.149	26	11/40	Surr 5/45†
U.150	26	11/40	Surr 5/45. To Ca
U.151	26	1/41	Sc 5/45
U.152	26	1/41	Sc 5/45
U.153	3	7/41	Lost 13/7/42
U.154	3	8/41	Lost 3/7/44
U.155	3	8/41	Surr 5/45†
U.156	3	9/41	Lost 8/3/43
U.157	3	9/41	Lost 13/6/42
U.158	3	9/41	Lost 30/6/42
U.159	3	10/41	Lost 15/7/43
U.160	3	10/41	Lost 14/7/43
U.161	53	7/41	Lost 27/9/43
U.162	53	9/41	Lost 3/9/42
U.163	53	10/41	Lost 21/3/43
U.164	53	11/41	Lost 6/1/43
U.165	53	2/42	Lost 22/3/43
U.166	53	3/42	Lost 1/8/42
U.167	53	7/42	Lost 5/4/43
U.168	53	9/42	Lost 5/10/44
U.169	53	11/42	Lost 27/4/43
U.170	53	1/43	Surr 5/45†
U.171	3	10/41	Lost 9/10/42
U.172	3	11/41	Lost 13/12/43
U.173	3	11/41	Lost 16/11/42
U.174	3	11/41	Lost 27/4/43
U.175	3	12/41	Lost 17/4/43
U.176	3	12/41	Lost 15/5/43
U.177	3	3/42	Lost 6/2/44
U.178	3	2/42	Sc 8/44
U.179	3	3/42	Lost 8/10/42
U.180	3	5/42	Lost 22/8/44
U.181	3	5/42	To Japan as *I.501*; qv.
U.182	3	6/42	Lost 16/5/43
U.183	3	4/42	Lost 23/4/45
U.184	3	5/42	Lost 20/11/42
U.185	3	6/42	Lost 24/8/43
U.186	3	7/42	Lost 12/5/43
U.187	3	7/42	Lost 4/2/43
U.188	3	8/42	Sc 8/44
U.189	3	8/42	Lost 23/4/43
U.190	3	9/42	Surr 5/45. To Ca
U.191	3	10/42	Lost 23/4/43
U.192	3	11/42	Lost 5/5/43
U.193	3	12/42	Lost 28/4/44
U.194	3	1/43	Lost 24/6/43
U.195	3	9/42	To Japan *I.506* qv.
U.196	3	9/42	Lost 30/11/44
U.197	3	10/42	Lost 20/8/43
U.198	3	11/42	Lost 12/8/44
U.199	3	11/42	Lost 31/7/43
U.200	3	12/42	Lost 24/6/43
U.201	30	1/41	Lost 17/2/43
U.202	30	3/41	Lost 1/6/43
U.203	30	2/41	Lost 25/4/43
U.204	30	3/41	Lost 19/10/41
U.205	30	5/41	Lost 17/2/43
U.206	30	5/41	Lost 30/11/41
U.207	30	6/41	Lost 11/9/41
U.208	30	7/41	Lost 11/12/41
U.209	30	10/41	Lost 19/5/43
U.210	30	2/42	Lost 6/8/42
U.211	30	3/42	Lost 19/11/43
U.212	30	4/42	Lost 21/7/44
U.213	30	8/41	Lost 31/7/42
U.214	30	11/41	Lost 26/7/44
U.215	30	11/41	Lost 3/7/42
U.216	30	12/41	Lost 20/10/42
U.217	30	1/42	Lost 5/6/43
U.218	30	1/42	Surr 5/45†
U.219	30	12/42	To Japan, *I.505* qv
U.220	30	3/43	Lost 28/10/43
U.221	30	5/42	Lost 27/9/43
U.222	30	5/42	MC 2/9/42
U.223	30	6/42	Lost 30/3/44
U.224	30	6/42	Lost 13/1/43
U.225	30	7/42	Lost 21/2/43
U.226	30	8/42	Lost 6/11/43
U.227	30	8/42	Lost 30/4/43
U.228	30	9/42	Lost 4/10/44
U.229	30	10/42	Lost 22/9/43
U.230	30	10/42	Sc Toulon 21/8/44
U.231	30	11/42	Lost 13/1/44
U.232	30	11/42	Lost 8/7/43
U.233	30	9/43	Lost 5/7/44
U.234	30	3/44	Surr 5/45. To US
U.235	30	12/42	MC 14/4/45
U.236	30	1/43	Lost 4/5/45
U.237	30	1/43	Lost 4/4/45
U.238	30	2/43	Lost 9/2/44
U.239	30	3/43	Lost 23/7/44
U.240	30	4/43	Lost 16/5/44
U.241	30	7/43	Lost 18/5/44
U.242	30	8/43	Lost 30/4/45
U.243	30	10/43	Lost 8/7/44
U.244	30	10/43	Surr 5/45†
U.245	30	12/43	Surr 5/45†
U.246	30	1/44	Lost 29/3/45
U.247	30	10/43	Lost 1/9/44
U.248	30	11/43	Lost 16/1/45
U.249	30	11/43	Surr 5/45†
U.250	30	12/43	Lost 30/7/44
U.251	6	9/41	Lost 19/4/45
U.252	6	10/41	Lost 14/4/42
U.253	6	10/41	Lost 23/9/42
U.254	6	11/41	MC 8/12/42
U.255	6	11/41	Surr 5/45†
U.256	6	12/41	Surr 5/45 Sc.
U.257	6	1/42	Lost 24/2/44
U.258	6	2/42	Lost 20/5/43
U.259	6	2/42	Lost 15/11/42
U.260	6	3/42	Lost 12/3/45
U.261	6	3/42	Lost 15/9/42
U.262	6	4/42	Surr 5/45. Sc
U.263	6	5/42	Lost 20/1/44
U.264	6	5/42	Lost 19/2/44
U.265	6	6/42	Lost 3/2/43
U.266	6	6/42	Lost 14/5/43
U.267	6	7/42	Sc 5/45
U.268	6	7/42	Lost 19/2/43
U.269	6	8/42	Lost 25/6/44
U.270	6	9/42	Lost 13/8/44
U.271	6	9/42	Lost 28/1/44
U.272	6	10/42	MC 12/11/42
U.273	6	10/42	Lost 19/5/43
U.274	6	11/42	Lost 23/10/43
U.275	6	11/42	Lost 10/3/45
U.276	6	12/42	Surr 5/45. Sc
U.277	6	12/42	Lost 1/5/44
U.278	6	1/43	Surr 5/45†
U.279	6	2/43	Lost 4/10/43
U.280	6	2/43	Lost 16/11/43
U.281	6	2/43	Surr 5/45†
U.282	6	3/43	Lost 29/10/43
U.283	6	3/43	Lost 11/2/44
U.284	6	4/43	Lost 21/12/43
U.285	6	5/43	Lost 15/4/45
U.286	6	6/43	Lost 29/4/45
U.287	6	9/43	Sc 5/45
U.288	6	6/43	Lost 3/4/44
U.289	6	7/43	Lost 31/5/44
U.290	6	7/43	Sc 5/45
U.291	6	8/43	Surr 5/45†
U.292	6	8/43	Lost 27/5/44
U.293	6	9/43	Surr 5/45†
U.294	6	10/43	Surr 5/45†
U.295	6	10/43	Surr 5/45†
U.296	6	11/43	Lost 22/3/45
U.297	6	11/43	Lost 6/12/44
U.298	6	12/43	Surr 5/45†
U.299	6	12/43	Surr 5/45†
U.300	6	12/43	Lost 22/2/45
U.301	27	5/42	Lost 21/1/43
U.302	27	6/42	Lost 6/4/44
U.303	27	7/42	Lost 21/5/43
U.304	27	8/42	Lost 28/5/43
U.305	27	9/42	Lost 17/1/44
U.306	27	10/42	Lost 31/10/43
U.307	27	11/42	Lost 29/4/45
U.308	27	12/42	Lost 4/6/43
U.309	27	1/43	Lost 16/2/45
U.310	27	2/43	Surr 5/45. BU
U.311	27	3/43	Lost 24/4/44
U.312	27	4/43	Surr 5/45†
U.313	27	5/43	Surr 5/45†
U.314	27	6/43	Lost 30/1/44
U.315	27	7/43	Surr 5/45. BU
U.316	27	8/43	Sc 5/45
U.317	27	10/43	Lost 26/6/44
U.318	27	11/43	Surr 5/45†
U.319	27	12/43	Lost 15/7/44
U.320	27	12/43	Lost 7/5/45
U.321	27	1/44	Lost 2/4/45
U.322	27	2/44	Lost 25/11/44
U.323	27	3/44	Sc 5/45
U.324	27	4/44	Surr 5/45. BU
U.325	27	5/44	Lost 30/4/45
U.326	27	6/44	Lost 4/45
U.327	27	7/44	Lost 27/2/45
U.328	27	9/44	Surr 5/456
U.329	27	10/44	Lost 30/3/45
U.330	27	—	Canc
U.331	44	3/41	Lost 17/11/42
U.332	44	6/41	Lost 2/5/43
U.333	44	8/41	Lost 31/7/44
U.334	44	10/41	Lost 14/6/43
U.335	44	12/41	Lost 3/8/42
U.336	44	2/42	Lost 4/10/43
U.337	44	5/42	Lost 15/1/43
U.338	44	6/42	Lost 20/9/43
U.339	44	8/42	Sc 5/45
U.340	44	10/42	Lost 1/11/43
U.341	44	11/42	Lost 19/9/43
U.342	44	1/43	Lost 17/4/44
U.343	44	2/43	Lost 10/3/44
U.344	44	3/43	Lost 24/8/44
U.345	44	5/43	Lost 13/12/43
U.346	44	6/43	MC 20/9/43
U.347	44	7/43	Lost 17/4/44
U.348	44	8/43	Lost 30/3/45
U.349	44	9/43	Sc 5/45
U.350	28	10/43	Lost 30/3/45
U.351	28	6/41	Sc 5/45
U.352	28	8/41	Lost 9/5/42
U.353	28	3/42	Lost 16/10/42
U.354	28	4/42	Lost 25/8/44
U.355	28	10/41	Lost 1/4/44

Name	Builder	In Service	Fate
U.356	28	12/41	Lost 27/12/42
U.357	28	6/42	Lost 26/12/42
U.358	28	8/42	Lost 1/3/44
U.359	28	10/42	Lost 28/7/43
U.360	28	11/42	Lost 2/4/44
U.361	28	12/42	Lost 17/7/44
U.362	28	2/43	Lost 5/9/44
U.363	28	3/43	Surr 5/45†
U.364	28	5/43	Lost 30/1/44
U.365	28	6/43	Lost 13/12/44
U.366	28	7/43	Lost 5/3/44
U.367	28	8/43	Lost 15/3/45
U.368	28	1/44	Surr 5/45†
U.369	28	10/43	Surr 5/45†
U.370	28	11/43	Sc 5/45
U.371	33	3/41	Lost 4/5/44
U.372	33	4/41	Lost 4/8/42
U.373	33	5/41	Lost 8/6/44
U.374	33	6/41	Lost 12/1/42
U.375	33	7/41	Lost 30/7/43
U.376	33	8/41	Lost 10/4/43
U.377	33	10/41	Lost 15/1/44
U.378	33	10/41	Lost 20/10/43
U.379	33	11/41	Lost 8/8/42
U.380	33	12/41	Lost 11/3/44
U.381	33	2/42	Lost 19/5/43
U.382	33	4/42	MC 1/45
U.383	33	6/42	Lost 1/8/43
U.384	33	7/42	Lost 20/3/43
U.385	33	8/42	Lost 11/8/44
U.386	33	10/42	Lost 19/2/44
U.387	33	11/42	Lost 9/12/44
U.388	33	12/42	Lost 20/6/43
U.389	33	2/43	Lost 5/10/43
U.390	33	3/43	Lost 5/7/44
U.391	33	4/43	Lost 13/12/43
U.392	33	5/43	Lost 16/3/44
U.393	33	7/43	Lost 4/5/45
U.394	33	8/43	Lost 2/9/44
U.395	33	—	Canc
U.396	33	10/43	Lost 23/4/45
U.397	33	11/43	Sc 5/45
U.398	33	12/43	Lost 4/45
U.399	33	1/44	Lost 26/3/45
U.400	33	3/44	Lost 17/12/44
U.401	18	4/41	Lost 3/8/41
U.402	18	5/41	Lost 13/10/43
U.403	18	6/41	Lost 17/8/43
U.404	18	8/41	Lost 28/7/43
U.405	18	9/41	Lost 1/11/43
U.406	18	10/41	Lost 18/2/44
U.407	18	12/41	Lost 19/9/44
U.408	18	11/41	Lost 5/11/42
U.409	18	1/42	Lost 12/7/43
U.410	18	2/42	Lost 11/3/44
U.411	18	3/42	Lost 15/11/42
U.412	18	4/42	Lost 22/10/42
U.413	18	6/42	Lost 20/8/44
U.414	18	7/42	Lost 25/5/43
U.415	18	8/42	Lost 14/7/44
U.416	18	11/42	Lost 30/3/43
U.417	18	9/42	Lost 11/6/43
U.418	18	10/42	Lost 1/6/43
U.419	18	11/42	Lost 8/10/43
U.420	18	12/42	Lost 26/10/43
U.421	18	1/43	Lost 29/4/44
U.422	18	2/43	Lost 4/10/43
U.423	18	3/43	Lost 17/6/44
U.424	18	4/43	Lost 11/2/44
U.425	18	4/43	Lost 17/2/45
U.426	18	5/43	Lost 8/1/44
U.427	18	6/43	Surr 5/45†
U.428	18	/43	To Italy, *S.3* qv Sc 5/45
U.429	18	/43	To Italy, *S.4* qv Lost 30/3/45
U.430	18	/43	To Italy, *S.6* qv Lost 30/3/45
U.431	50	4/41	Lost 30/10/43
U.432	50	4/41	Lost 11/3/43
U.433	50	5/41	Lost 16/11/41
U.434	50	6/41	Lost 18/12/41
U.435	50	8/41	Lost 9/7/43
U.436	50	9/41	Lost 26/5/43
U.437	50	10/41	Lost 4/10/44
U.438	50	11/41	Lost 6/5/43
U.439	50	12/41	MC 3/5/43
U.440	50	1/42	Lost 31/5/43
U.441	50	2/42	Lost 18/6/44
U.442	50	3/42	Lost 12/2/43
U.443	50	4/42	Lost 23/2/43
U.444	50	5/42	Lost 11/3/43
U.445	50	5/42	Lost 24/8/44
U.446	50	6/42	Lost 21/9/42
U.447	50	7/42	Lost 7/5/43
U.448	50	8/42	Lost 14/4/44
U.449	50	8/42	Lost 24/6/43
U.450	50	9/42	Lost 10/3/44
U.451	26	5/41	Lost 21/12/41
U.452	26	5/41	Lost 25/8/41
U.453	26	6/41	Lost 21/5/44
U.454	26	7/41	Lost 1/8/43
U.455	26	8/41	Lost 6/4/44
U.456	26	9/41	Lost 13/5/43
U.457	26	11/41	Lost 16/9/42
U.458	26	12/41	Lost 22/8/43
U.459	26	11/41	Lost 24/7/43
U.460	26	12/41	Lost 4/10/43
U.461	26	1/42	Lost 30/7/43
U.462	26	3/42	Lost 30/7/43
U.463	26	4/42	Lost 15/5/43
U.464	26	4/42	Lost 20/8/42
U.465	26	5/42	Lost 7/5/43
U.466	26	6/42	Sc 8/44
U.467	26	7/42	Lost 25/5/43
U.468	26	8/42	Lost 11/8/43
U.469	26	10/42	Lost 25/3/43
U.470	26	1/43	Lost 16/10/43
U.471	26	5/43	Lost 6/8/44. Fr *Mille*, 1963
U.472	26	5/43	Lost 4/3/44
U.473	26	6/43	Lost 5/5/44
U.474	26	—	Lost 1944
U.475	26	7/43	Sc 5/45
U.476	26	7/43	Lost 24/5/44
U.477	26	8/43	Lost 3/6/44
U.478	26	9/43	Lost 30/6/44
U.479	26	10/43	Lost 12/12/44
U.480	26	10/43	Lost 24/2/45
U.481	26	11/43	Surr 5/45†
U.482	26	12/43	Lost 16/1/45
U.483	26	12/43	Surr 5/45†
U.484	26	1/44	Lost 9/9/44
U.485	26	2/44	Surr 5/45†
U.486	26	3/44	Lost 12/4/45
U.487	26	12/42	Lost 13/7/43
U.488	26	2/43	Lost 26/4/44
U.489	26	3/43	Lost 4/8/43
U.490	26	3/43	Lost 12/6/44
U.491-493	26	—	Canc
U.494-496	30	—	Canc
U.497-500	26	—	Canc
U.501	21	4/41	Lost 10/9/41
U.502	21	5/41	Lost 5/7/42
U.503	21	7/41	Lost 15/3/42
U.504	21	7/41	Lost 30/7/43
U.505	21	8/41	Captured USN 4/6/44
U.506	21	9/41	Lost 12/7/43
U.507	21	10/41	Lost 13/1/43
U.508	21	10/41	Lost 12/11/43
U.509	21	11/41	Lost 15/7/43
U.510	21	11/41	Surr 5/45. Fr *Bouan*, Str 1958
U.511	21	12/41	To Japan *Ro.500* qv
U.512	21	12/41	Lost 2/10/42
U.513	21	1/42	Lost 19/7/43
U.514	21	1/42	Lost 8/7/43
U.515	21	2/42	Lost 9/4/44
U.516	21	3/42	Surr 5/45†
U.517	21	3/42	Lost 21/11/42
U.518	21	4/42	Lost 22/4/45
U.519	21	5/42	Lost 10/2/43
U.520	21	5/42	Lost 30/10/42
U.521	21	6/42	Lost 2/6/43
U.522	21	6/42	Lost 23/2/43
U.523	21	6/42	Lost 25/8/43
U.524	21	7/42	Lost 22/3/43
U.525	21	7/42	Lost 11/8/43
U.526	21	8/42	Lost 14/4/43
U.527	21	9/42	Lost 23/7/43
U.528	21	9/42	Lost 11/5/43
U.529	21	9/42	Lost 15/2/43
U.530	21	10/42	Surr 5/45. To US
U.531	21	10/42	Lost 6/5/43
U.532	21	11/42	Surr 5/45†
U.533	21	11/42	Lost 16/10/43
U.534	21	12/42	Lost 5/5/45
U.535	21	12/42	Lost 5/7/43
U.536	21	1/43	Lost 20/11/43
U.537	21	1/43	Lost 9/11/44
U.538	21	2/43	Lost 21/11/43
U.539	21	2/43	Surr 5/45†
U.540	21	3/43	Lost 17/10/43
U.541	21	3/43	Surr 5/45†
U.542	21	4/43	Lost 28/11/43
U.543	21	4/43	Lost 2/7/44
U.544	21	5/43	Lost 16/1/44
U.545	21	5/43	Lost 10/2/44
U.546	21	6/43	Lost 24/4/45
U.547	21	6/43	Lost 11/44
U.548	21	6/43	Lost 30/4/45
U.549	21	7/43	Lost 29/5/44
U.550	21	7/43	Lost 16/4/44
U.551	5	11/40	Lost 23/3/41
U.552	5	12/40	Sc 5/45
U.553	5	12/40	Lost 28/1/43
U.554	5	1/41	Sc 5/45
U.555	5	1/41	Surr 5/45. BU
U.556	5	2/41	Lost 27/6/41
U.557	5	2/41	Lost 16/12/41
U.558	5	2/41	Lost 20/7/43
U.559	5	2/41	Lost 30/10/42
U.560	5	3/41	MC 11/41
U.561	5	3/41	Lost 12/7/43
U.562	5	3/41	Lost 19/2/43
U.563	5	3/41	Lost 31/5/43
U.564	5	4/41	Lost 14/6/43
U.565	5	4/41	Lost 24/9/44
U.566	5	4/41	Lost 24/10/43
U.567	5	4/41	Lost 21/12/41
U.568	5	5/41	Lost 28/5/42
U.569	5	5/41	Lost 22/5/43
U.570	5	5/41	Captured UK 27/8/41. (RN *Graph*)

Name	Builder	In Service	Fate
U.571	5	5/41	Lost 28/1/44
U.572	5	5/41	Lost 3/8/43
U.573	5	6/41	Int Spain 1/5/42 (Sp *G.7*)
U.574	5	6/41	Lost 19/12/41
U.575	5	6/41	Lost 13/3/44
U.576	5	6/41	Lost 15/7/42
U.577	5	7/41	Lost 9/1/42
U.578	5	7/41	Lost 10/8/42
U.579	5	7/41	Lost 5/5/45
U.580	5	7/41	MC 11/11/41
U.581	5	7/41	Lost 2/2/42
U.582	5	8/41	Lost 5/10/42
U.583	5	8/41	MC 15/11/41
U.584	5	8/41	Lost 31/10/43
U.585	5	8/41	Lost 29/3/42
U.586	5	9/41	Lost 5/7/44
U.587	5	9/41	Lost 27/3/42
U.588	5	9/41	Lost 31/7/42
U.589	5	9/41	Lost 14/9/42
U.590	5	10/41	Lost 9/7/43
U.591	5	10/41	Lost 30/7/43
U.592	5	10/41	Lost 31/1/44
U.593	5	10/41	Lost 13/12/43
U.594	5	10/41	Lost 4/6/43
U.595	5	11/41	Lost 14/11/42
U.596	5	11/41	Lost 24/9/44
U.597	5	11/41	Lost 12/10/42
U.598	5	11/41	Lost 23/7/43
U.599	5	12/41	Lost 24/10/42
U.600	5	12/41	Lost 25/11/43
U.601	5	12/41	Lost 25/2/44
U.602	5	12/41	Lost 23/4/43
U.603	5	1/42	Lost 1/3/44
U.604	5	1/42	Lost 3/8/43
U.605	5	1/42	Lost 13/11/42
U.606	5	1/42	Lost 22/2/43
U.607	5	1/42	Lost 13/7/43
U.608	5	2/42	Lost 19/8/44
U.609	5	2/42	Lost 7/2/43
U.610	5	2/42	Lost 8/10/43
U.611	5	2/42	Lost 10/12/42
U.612	5	3/42	Sc 5/45
U.613	5	3/42	Lost 23/7/43
U.614	5	3/42	Lost 29/7/43
U.615	5	3/42	Lost 7/8/43
U.616	5	4/42	Lost 14/5/44
U.617	5	4/42	Lost 11/9/43
U.618	5	4/42	Lost 14/8/44
U.619	5	4/42	Lost 15/10/42
U.620	5	4/42	Lost 14/2/43
U.621	5	5/42	Lost 18/8/44
U.622	5	5/42	Lost 24/7/43
U.623	5	5/42	Lost 21/2/43
U.624	5	5/42	Lost 7/2/43
U.625	5	6/42	Lost 10/3/44
U.626	5	6/42	Lost 15/12/42
U.627	5	6/42	Lost 27/10/42
U.628	5	6/42	Lost 3/7/43
U.629	5	7/42	Lost 8/6/44
U.630	5	7/42	Lost 4/5/43
U.631	5	7/42	Lost 17/10/43
U.632	5	7/42	Lost 6/4/43
U.633	5	7/42	Lost 7/3/43
U.634	5	8/42	Lost 30/8/43
U.635	5	8/42	Lost 6/4/43
U.636	5	8/42	Lost 21/4/45
U.637	5	8/42	Surr 5/45†
U.638	5	9/42	Lost 6/5/43
U.639	5	9/42	Lost 30/8/43
U.640	5	9/42	Lost 17/5/43
U.641	5	9/42	Lost 19/1/44
U.642	5	10/42	Lost 5/7/44
U.643	5	10/42	Lost 8/10/43
U.644	5	10/42	Lost 7/4/43
U.645	5	10/42	Lost 24/12/43
U.646	5	10/42	Lost 17/5/43
U.647	5	11/42	Lost 3/8/43
U.648	5	11/42	Lost 23/11/43
U.649	5	11/42	MC 24/2/43
U.650	5	11/42	Lost 12/44
U.651	34	2/41	Lost 29/6/41
U.652	34	4/41	Lost 2/6/42
U.653	34	5/41	Lost 15/3/44
U.654	34	7/41	Lost 22/8/42
U.655	34	8/41	Lost 24/3/42
U.656	34	9/41	Lost 1/3/42
U.657	34	10/41	Lost 17/5/43
U.658	34	11/41	Lost 30/10/42
U.659	34	12/41	MC 3/5/43
U.660	34	1/42	Lost 12/11/42
U.661	34	2/42	Lost 15/10/42
U.662	34	4/42	Lost 21/7/43
U.663	34	5/42	Lost 7/5/43
U.664	34	6/42	Lost 9/8/43
U.665	34	7/42	Lost 22/3/43
U.666	34	8/42	Lost 10/2/44
U.667	34	10/42	Lost 25/8/44
U.668	34	11/42	Surr 5/45†
U.669	34	12/42	Lost 7/9/43
U.670	34	1/43	MC 21/8/43
U.671	34	3/43	Lost 4/8/44
U.672	34	4/43	Lost 18/7/44
U.673	34	5/43	MC 16/10/44
U.674	34	6/43	Lost 2/5/44
U.675	34	7/43	Lost 24/544
U.676	34	8/43	Lost 19/12/45
U.677	34	9/43	Lost 8/4/45
U.678	34	10/43	Lost 6/7/44
U.679	34	11/43	Lost 10/1/45
U.680	34	12/43	Surr 5/45†
U.681	34	2/44	Lost 11/3/45
U.682	34	4/44	Lost 31/3/45
U.683	34	5/44	Lost 12/3/45
U.684-686	34	—	Canc
U.687-700	34	—	Projected
U.701	55	7/41	Lost 7/7/42
U.702	55	9/41	Lost 4/4/42
U.703	55	10/41	Lost 30/9/44
U.704	55	11/41	Sc 3/5/45
U.705	55	12/41	Lost 3/9/42
U.706	55	3/42	Lost 2/8/43
U.707	55	7/42	Lost 9/11/43
U.708	55	7/42	Sc 5/45
U.709	55	8/42	Lost 1/3/44
U.710	55	9/42	Lost 24/4/43
U.711	55	9/42	Lost 4/5/45
U.712	55	11/42	Surr 5/45. To UK, BU 1950
U.713	55	12/42	Lost 24/2/44
U.714	55	2/43	Lost 14/3/45
U.715	55	3/43	Lost 13/6/44
U.716	55	4/43	Surr 5/45
U.717	55	5/43	Lost 2/5/45
U.718	55	6/43	MC 18/11/43
U.719	55	7/43	Lost 26/6/44
U.720	55	9/43	Surr 5/45†
U.721	55	11/43	Sc 5/45
U.722	55	12/43	Lost 27/3/45
U.723-730	55	—	Canc
U.731	50	10/42	Lost 15/5/44
U.732	50	10/42	Lost 31/10/43
U.733	50	11/42	Lost 5/5/45
U.734	50	12/42	Lost 9/2/44
U.735	50	12/42	Lost 28/12/44
U.736	50	1/43	Lost 6/8/44
U.737	50	1/43	MC 19/12/44
U.738	50	2/43	MC 14/2/44
U.739	50	3/43	Surr 5/45†
U.740	50	3/43	Lost 9/6/44
U.741	50	4/43	Lost 15/8/44
U.742	50	5/43	Lost 18/7/44
U.743	50	5/43	Lost 9/9/44
U.744	50	6/43	Lost 6/3/44
U.745	50	7/43	Lost 4/2/45
U.746	50	7/43	To Italy as *S.2* qv Sc 5/45
U.747	50	7/43	To Italy as *S.3* qv Lost 8/4/45
U.748	50	7/43	To Italy as *S.5* qv Sc 5/45
U.749	50	8/43	To Italy as *S.7* qv Lost 4/4/45
U.750	50	8/43	To Italy as *S.9* qv Sc 5/45
U.751	58	1/41	Lost 17/7/42
U.752	58	5/41	Lost 23/5/43
U.753	58	6/41	Lost 13/5/43
U.754	58	8/41	Lost 31/7/42
U.755	58	11/41	Lost 28/5/43
U.756	58	12/41	Lost 3/9/42
U.757	58	2/42	Lost 8/1/44
U.758	58	5/42	Surr 5/45. BU
U.759	58	8/42	Lost 26/7/43
U.760	58	10/42	Int Vigo 8/9/43. Surr, Sc.
U.761	58	12/42	Lost 24/2/44
U.762	58	1/43	Lost 8/2/44
U.763	58	3/43	Lost 24/1/45
U.764	58	5/43	Surr 5/45†
U.765	58	6/43	Lost 6/5/44
U.766	58	7/43	Surr 5/45. Fr *Laubie*, Str 1961
U.767	58	9/43	Lost 18/6/44
U.768	58	10/43	MC 20/11/43
U.769-770	58	—	B 20/11/43. CTL
U.771	58	11/43	Lost 11/11/44
U.772	58	12/43	Lost 30/12/44
U.773	58	1/44	Surr 5/45†
U.774	58	2/44	Lost 8/4/45
U.775	58	3/44	Surr 5/45†
U.776	58	4/44	Surr 5/45†
U.777	58	5/44	Lost 15/10/44
U.778	58	7/44	Surr 5/45†
U.779	58	8/44	Surr 5/45†
U.780-784	58	—	Canc
U.785	58	—	Lost 1945
U.786-790	58	—	Canc
U.791	30	—	BU incomplete
U.792	5	11/43	Sc 5/45. To UK, BU
U.793	5	1/44	Sc 5/45. To UK, BU
U.794	30	11/43	Sc 5/45
U.795	30	1945	Sc 5/45. To UK, BU
U.796-797	30	—	Canc, BU 4/44
U.798	30	—	BU incomplete
U.799-800	30	—	Canc
U.801	53	3/43	Lost 16/3/44
U.802	53	6/43	Surr 5/45†

U.803	53	9/43	Lost 27/4/44
U.804	53	12/43	Lost 9/4/45
U.805	53	2/44	Surr 5/45. Sc.
U.806	53	4/44	Surr 5/45. BU
U.807-816	53	—	Canc
U.817-820	53	—	Projected
U.821	46	10/43	Lost 10/6/44
U.822	46	7/44	Sc 5/45
U.823-824	46	—	Canc
U.825	50	5/44	Surr 5/45†
U.826	50	5/44	Surr 5/45†
U.827	50	5/44	Sc 5/45
U.828	50	6/44	Sc 5/45
U.829-834	50	—	Canc
U.835	50		Sc 5/45
U.836	50		Sc 5/45
U.837-840	50	—	Canc
U.841	3	2/43	Lost 17/10/43
U.842	3	3/43	Lost 6/11/43
U.843	3	3/43	Lost 9/4/45
U.844	3	4/43	Lost 16/10/43
U.845	3	5/43	Lost 10/3/44
U.846	3	5/43	Lost 4/5/44
U.847	3	1/43	Lost 27/8/43
U.848	3	2/43	Lost 5/11/43
U.849	3	3/43	Lost 25/11/43
U.850	3	4/43	Lost 20/12/43
U.851	3	5/43	Lost 3/44
U.852	3	6/43	Lost 3/5/44
U.853	3	6/43	Lost 6/5/45
U.854	3	7/43	Lost 4/2/44
U.855	3	8/43	Lost 24/9/44
U.856	3	8/43	Lost 7/4/44
U.857	3	9/43	Lost 7/4/45
U.858	3	9/43	Surr 5/45. To US
U.859	3	7/43	Lost 23/9/44
U.860	3	8/43	Lost 15/6/44
U.861	3	9/43	Surr 5/45†
U.862	3	10/43	Trf Japan as *I.502* qv
U.863	3	11/43	Lost 29/9/44
U.864	3	12/43	Lost 9/2/45
U.865	3	10/43	Lost 19/9/44
U.866	3	11/43	Lost 18/3/45
U.867	3	12/43	Lost 19/9/44
U.868	3	12/43	Surr 5/45†
U.869	3	1/44	Lost 28/2/45
U.870	3	2/44	Lost 30/3/45
U.871	3	1/44	Lost 26/9/44
U.872	3	2/44	Lost 29/7/44
U.873	3	3/44	Surr 5/45. To US BU
U.874	3	4/44	Surr 5/45†
U.875	3	4/44	Surr 5/45†
U.876	3	5/44	Lost 4/5/45
U.877	3	3/44	Lost 27/12/44
U.878	3	4/44	Lost 10/4/45
U.879	3	4/44	Lost 19/4/45
U.880	3	5/44	Lost 16/4/45
U.881	3	5/44	Lost 6/5/45
U.882	3	—	Canc
U.883	3	3/45	Surr 5/45†
U.884	3	—	Lost 30/3/45
U.885	3	—	Canc
U.886	3	—	Lost 30/3/45
U.887-888	3	—	Canc
U.889	3	8/44	Surr 5/45. To US 1946
U.890-892	3	—	Lost 29/7/44
U.893-894	3	—	Canc
U.895-900	3	—	Canc
U.901	2	4/44	Surr 5/45†
U.902	2	—	Canc
U.903	27	9/43	Sc 5/45
U.904	27	9/43	Lost 4/5/45
U.905	55	3/44	Lost 20/3/45
U.906	55	7/44	Lost 31/12/44
U.907	55	5/44	Surr 5/45†
U.908	55	—	Lost 31/12/44
U.909-918	55	—	Canc
U.919-920	55	—	Projected
U.921	43	5/43	Lost 30/9/44
U.922	43	8/43	Sc 5/45
U.923	43	10/43	Lost 2/45
U.924	43	11/43	Sc 5/45
U.925	43	12/43	Lost 18/9/44
U.926	43	2/44	Surr 5/45. To No as *Kya* 1948, BU 1964
U.927	43	6/44	Lost 24/2/45
U.928	43	7/44	Surr 5/45†
U.929	43	9/44	Sc 5/45
U.930	43	12/44	Surr 5/45†
U.931-942	43	—	Canc
U.943-950	43	—	Projected
U.951	5	12/42	Lost 7/7/43
U.952	5	12/42	Lost 6/8/44
U.953	5	12/42	Surr 5/45, To UK, BU 1949
U.954	5	12/42	Lost 19/5/43
U.955	5	12/42	Lost 7/6/44
U.956	5	1/43	Surr 5/45†
U.957	5	1/43	MC 19/10/44
U.958	5	1/43	Sc 5/45
U.959	5	1/43	Lost 2/5/44
U.960	5	1/44	Lost 19/5/44
U.961	5	2/43	Lost 29/3/44
U.962	5	2/43	Lost 8/4/44
U.963	5	2/43	MC 9/5/45
U.964	5	2/43	Lost 16/10/43
U.965	5	2/43	Lost 27/3/45
U.966	5	3/43	Lost 10/11/43
U.967	5	3/43	Sc 8/44
U.968	5	3/43	Surr 5/45†
U.969	5	3/43	Lost 6/8/44
U.970	5	3/43	Lost 7/6/44
U.971	5	4/43	Lost 24/6/44
U.972	5	4/43	Lost 1/44
U.973	5	4/43	Lost 6/3/44
U.974	5	4/43	Lost 19/4/44
U.975	5	4/43	Surr 5/45†
U.976	5	5/43	Lost 25/3/44
U.977	5	5/43	Surr 5/45. Sc
U.978	5	5/43	Surr 5/45†
U.979	5	5/43	Sc 5/45
U.980	5	5/43	Lost 11/6/44
U.981	5	6/43	Lost 12/8/44
U.982	5	6/43	Lost 8/4/45
U.983	5	6/43	MC 8/9/43
U.984	5	6/43	Lost 20/8/44
U.985	5	6/43	Lost 23/10/44
U.986	5	7/43	Lost 17/4/44
U.987	5	7/43	Lost 5/6/44
U.988	5	7/43	Lost 29/6/44
U.989	5	7/43	Lost 14/2/45
U.990	5	7/43	Lost 25/5/44
U.991	5	7/43	Surr 5/45†
U.992	5	8/43	Surr 5/45†
U.993	5	8/43	Lost 4/10/44
U.994	5	9/43	Surr 5/45†
U.995	5	9/43	Surr 5/45. To No as *Kaura* 1948, war memorial 1963
U.996	5	—	Lost 8/44
U.997	5	9/43	Surr 5/45†
U.998	5	10/43	Lost 16/6/44
U.999	5	10/43	Sc 5/45
U.1000	5	11/43	Lost 25/8/44
U.1001	5	11/43	Lost 8/4/45
U.1002	5	11/43	Surr 5/45†
U.1003	5	12/43	Lost 20/3/45
U.1004	5	12/43	Surr 5/45†
U.1005	5	12/43	Surr 5/45†
U.1006	5	1/44	Lost 16/10/44
U.1007	5	1/44	Lost 2/5/45
U.1008	5	2/44	Lost 6/5/45
U.1009	5	2/44	Surr 5/45†
U.1010	5	2/44	Surr 5/45†
U.1011-1012	5	—	Lost 1944
U.1013	5	3/44	MC 17/3/44
U.1014	5	3/44	Lost 4/2/45
U.1015	5	3/44	MC 19/5/44
U.1016	5	4/44	Sc 5/45
U.1017	5	4/44	Lost 29/4/45
U.1018	5	4/44	Lost 27/2/45
U.1019	5	5/44	Surr 5/45†
U.1020	5	5/44	Lost 1/45
U.1021	5	5/44	Lost 30/3/45
U.1022	5	6/44	Surr 5/45†
U.1023	5	6/44	Surr 5/45. To UK Sc 1946
U.1024	5	6/44	Lost 12/4/45
U.1025	5	/44	Sc 5/45
U.1026-1031	5	—	Sc 5/45
U.1032-1046	5	—	Canc
U.1047	5	—	Sc 5/45. To UK
U.1048-1050	5	—	Canc
U.1051	30	3/44	Lost 27/1/45
U.1052	30	1/44	Surr 5/45†
U.1053	30	2/44	MC 15/2/45
U.1054	30	3/44	Surr 5/45. BU
U.1055	30	4/44	Lost 30/4/45
U.1056	30	4/44	Sc 5/45
U.1057	30	5/44	Surr 5/45. To USSR as *S.81*, Str 1963
U.1058	30	6/44	Su 5/45. To USSR as *S.82*, Str 1963
U.1059	30	5/43	Lost 19/3/44
U.1060	30	5/43	Lost 27/10/44
U.1061	30	8/43	Surr 5/45†
U.1062	30	6/43	Lost 30/9/44
U.1063	30	7/44	Lost 15/4/45
U.1064	30	7/44	Surr 5/45. To USSR *S.83*, Str 1963
U.1065	30	9/44	Lost 9/4/45
U.1066-1100	30	—	Canc
U.1101	44	11/43	Sc 5/45
U.1102	44	2/44	Surr 5/45†
U.1103	44	1/44	Surr 5/45†
U.1104	44	3/44	Surr 5/45. BU
U.1105	44	5/45	Surr 5/45. To US 1946
U.1106	44	7/44	Lost 29/3/45
U.1107	44	8/44	Lost 25/4/45
U.1108	44	11/44	Surr 5/45. To UK 1946, BU 1949

Name	Builder	In Service	Fate
U.1109	44	8/44	Surr 5/45. To UK 1947, BU 1949
U.1110	44	9/44	Surr 5/45†
U.111-1120	44	—	Canc
U.1121-1130	44	—	Projected
U.1131	33	5/44	Lost 9/4/45
U.1132	33	6/44	Sc 5/45
U.1133-1152	33	—	Canc
U.1153-1160	33	—	Projected
U.1161	18	8/43	To Italy as *S.8* qv Sc 5/45
U.1162	18	9/43	To Italy as
U.1163	18	10/43	*S.10* qv Sc 5/45
U.1164	18	10/43	Surr 5/45†
U.1165	18	11/43	Lost 23/7/44
U.1166	18	12/43	Surr 5/45†
U.1167	18	12/43	MC 22/7/44
U.1168	18	1/44	Lost 30/3/45
U.1169	18	2/44	Sc 5/45
U.1170	18	3/44	Lost 5/4/45
U.1171	18	1/44	Sc 5/45
U.1172	18	4/44	Surr 5/45. To UK as *N.19* BU 1949
U.1173	18	—	Lost 26/1/45
			Canc
			Completed by USSR postwar
U.1174	18	—	Canc
U.1175	18	—	Completed by USSR postwar
U.1176-1177	18	—	
U.1178-1190	18	—	Canc
U.1191	50	9/43	Lost 25/6/44
U.1192	50	9/43	Sc 5/45
U.1193	50	10/43	Sc 5/45
U.1194	50	10/43	Surr 5/45†
U.1195	50	11/43	Lost 6/4/45
U.1196	50	11/43	MC 8/44
U.1197	50	12/43	Lost 25/4/45
U.1198	50	12/43	Surr 5/45†
U.1199	50	12/43	Lost 21/1/45
U.1200	50	1/44	Lost 11/11/44
U.1201	50	1/44	Surr 5/45. BU
U.1202	50	1/44	Surr 5/45. To No as *Kynn* 1948. Str 1961
U.1203	50	2/44	Surr 5/45†
U.1204	50	2/44	Sc 5/45
U.1205	50	3/44	Sc 5/45
U.1206	50	3/44	MC 14/4/45
U.1207	50	3/44	Sc 5/45
U.1208	50	4/44	Lost 20/2/45
U.1209	50	4/44	MC 18/12/44
U.1210	50	4/44	Lost 3/5/45
U.1211-1216	50	—	Canc
U.1217	50		Surr 5/45. BU
U.1218-1220	50	—	Canc
U.1221	21	8/43	Lost 3/4/45
U.1222	21	9/43	Lost 11/7/44
U.1223	21	10/43	Lost 28/4/45
U.1224	21	10/43	To Japan as *Ro.501* qv
U.1225	21	11/43	Lost 24/6/44
U.1226	21	11/43	MC 28/10/44
U.1227	21	12/43	Lost 9/4/45
U.1228	21	12/43	Surr 5/45. BU
U.1229	21	1/44	Lost 20/8/44
U.1230	21	1/44	Surr 5/45†
U.1231	21	2/44	Surr 5/45. To USSR as *N.25*, Str 1960
U.1232	21	3/44	Surr 5/45. BU
U.1233	21	3/44	Surr 5/45†
U.1234	21	4/44	MC 15/5/44. CTL
U.1235	21	5/44	Lost 15/4/45
U.1236	21		Sc 5/45
U.1237	21		Sc 5/45
U.1238	21		Sc 5/45
U.1239-1262	21	—	Canc
U.1263-1270	21	—	Projected
U.1271	6	1/44	Surr 5/45. BU
U.1272	6	1/44	Surr 5/45. BU
U.1273	6	2/44	Lost 17/2/45
U.1274	6	3/44	Lost 16/4/45
U.1275	6	3/44	Surr 5/45. BU
U.1276	6	4/44	Lost 3/4/45
U.1277	6	5/44	Sc 6/45
U.1278	6	5/44	Lost 17/2/45
U.1279	6	7/44	Lost 3/2/45
U.1280-1297	6	—	Canc
U.1298-1300	6	—	Projected
U.1301	28	2/44	Surr 5/45†
U.1302	28	5/44	Lost 7/3/45
U.1303	28	4/44	Sc 5/45
U.1304	28	9/44	Sc 5/45
U.1305	28	9/44	Surr 5/45. To USSR as *S.48*, Str 1963
U.1306	28	12/44	Sc 5/45
U.1307	28	11/44	Surr 5/45†
U.1308	28	1/45	Sc 5/45
U.1309-1318	28	—	Canc
U.1319-1330	28	—	Projected
U.1331-1350	27	—	Canc
U.1351-1400	5	—	Projected
U.1401-1404	5	—	Canc
U.1405	5	/44	Sc 5/45
U.1406	5	/44	Sc 5/45, To US 1946, BU 1948
U.1407	5	/44	Sc 5/45, To UK as *Meteorite*, BU 1949
U.1408	5	—	Canc BU 2/45
U.1409	5	—	Canc BU 2/45
U.1410	5	—	Canc BU 3/44
U.1411-1463	5	—	Canc
U.1464-1500	5	—	Projected
U.1501-1530	3	—	Canc
U.1531-1542	3	—	Canc
U.1543-1600	3	—	Projected
U.1601-1615	3	—	Canc
U.1616-1700	3	—	Projected
U.1701-1715	3	—	Canc
U.1716-1800	3	—	Projected
U.1801-1828	3	—	Canc
U.1829-1900	3	—	Projected
U.1901-1904	3	—	Canc
U.1905-2000	3	—	Projected
U.2001-2004	3	—	Canc
U.2005 2100	3	—	Projected
U.2101-2104	30	—	Canc
U.2105-2110	30	—	Projected
U.2111	30	5/44	Hecht midget
U.2112	30	6/44	Hecht midget
U.2113	30	6/44	Hecht midget
U.2114-2250	30	—	Canc
U.2251	54	7/44	
U.2252	54	7/44	
U.2253	54	7/44	
U.2254	54	7/44	
U.2255	54	7/44	
U.2256	54	7/44	
U.2257	54	7/44	
U.2258	54	8/44	
U.2259	54	8/44	
U.2260	54	8/44	
U.2261	54	8/44	
U.2262	54	8/44	
U.2263	54	8/44	
U.2264	54	8/44	
U.2275	54	8/44	
U.2266	54	8/44	
U.2267	54	8/44	
U.2268	54	8/44	
U.2269	54	8/44	
U.2270	54	8/44	
U.2271	54	8/44	
U.2272	54	8/44	
U.2273	54	8/44	
U.2274	54	8/44	
U.2275	54	8/44	
U.2276	54	8/44	
U.2277	54	8/44	
U.2278	54	8/44	
U.2279	54	8/44	
U.2280	54	8/44	
U.2281	54	8/44	
U.2283	54	8/44	
U.2284	54	8/44	
U.2285	54	8/44	
U.2286	54	8/44	
U.2287	54	8/44	
U.2288	54	8/44	
U.2289	54	8/44	
U.2290	54	8/44	
U.2291	54	8/44	
U.2292	54	8/44	
U.2293	54	8/44	
U.2294	54	8/44	
U.2295	54	8/44	
U.2296-2300	54	—	Canc
U.2301-2318	50	—	Canc

Name	Builder	In Service	Fate
U.2319-2320	50	—	Projected
U.2321	21	6/44	Surr 5/45†
U.2322	21	7/44	Surr 5/45†
U.2323	21	7/44	Lost 29/7/44
U.2324	21	7/44	Surr 5/45†
U.2325	21	8/44	Surr 5/45†
U.2326	21	8/44	Surr 5/45, To UK as *N.35*, Fr 1946, MC 6/12/46
U.2327	21	8/44	Sc 5/45
U.2328	21	8/44	Surr 5/45†
U.2329	21	9/44	Surr 5/45†
U.2330	21	9/44	Sc 5/45
U.2331	21	9/44	MC 10/44
U.2332	21	11/44	Sc 5/45
U.2333	21	12/44	Sc 5/45
U.2334	21	9/44	Surr 5/45†
U.2335	21	9/44	Surr 5/45†
U.2336	21	9/44	Surr 5/45†
U.2337	21	10/44	Surr 5/45†
U.2338	21	10/44	Lost 4/5/45
U.2339	21	11/44	Sc 5/45
U.2340	21	10/44	Lost 30/3/45
U.2341	21	10/44	Surr 5/45†
U.2342	21	11/44	Lost 26/12/44
U.2343	21	11/44	Sc 5/45
U.2344	21	11/44	MC 18/2/45
U.2345	21	11/44	Surr 5/45†
U.2346	21	11/44	Sc 5/45
U.2347	21	12/44	Sc 5/45
U.2348	21	12/44	Surr 5/45. To UK, BU 1949
U.2349	21	12/44	Sc 5/45
U.2350	21	12/44	Surr 5/45†
U.2351	21	12/44	Surr 5/45. BU
U.2352	21	1/45	Sc 5/45
U.2353	21	1/45	Surr 5/45, To USSR as *N.31*, Str 1953
U.2354	21	1/45	Surr 5/45†
U.2355	21	1/45	Sc 5/45
U.2356	21	1/45	Surr 5/45. BU
U.2357	21	1/45	Sc 5/45
U.2358	21	1/45	Sc 5/45
U.2359	21	1/45	Lost 2/5/45
U.2360	21	1/45	Sc 5/45
U.2361	21	2/45	Surr 5/45†
U.2362	21	2/45	Sc 5/45
U.2363	21	2/45	Surr 5/45†
U.2364	21	2/45	Sc 5/45
U.2365	21	3/45	Lost 5/5/45
U.2366	21	3/45	Sc 5/45
U.2367	21	3/45	MC 5/5/45
U.2368	21	4/45	Sc 5/45
U.2369	21	3/45	Sc 5/45
U.2370	21	4/45	Sc 5/45
U.2371	21	4/45	Sc 5/45
U.2372-2377	25	—	BU incomplete
U.2378-2400	25	—	Canc
U.2401-2430	20	—	Canc
U.2431-2445	23	—	Canc
U.2446-2460	24	—	Canc
U.2461-2500	24	—	Projected
U.2501	5	6/44	Sc 5/45
U.2502	5	7/44	Surr 5/45. BU
U.2503	5	8/44	Lost 4/5/45
U.2504	5	8/44	Sc 5/45
U.2505	5	11/44	Sc 5/45
U.2506	5	8/44	Surr 5/45. BU
U.2507	5	9/44	Sc 5/45
U.2508	5	9/44	Sc 5/45
U.2509	5	9/44	Lost 8/4/45
U.2510	5	9/44	Sc 5/45
U.2511	5	9/44	Surr 5/45. BU
U.2512	5	10/44	Sc 5/45
U.2513	5	10/44	Surr 5/45. To US 1946
U.2514	5	12/44	Lost 8/4/45
U.2515	5	10/44	Lost 11/3/45
U.2516	5	10/44	Lost 8/4/45
U.2517	5	10/44	Sc 5/45
U.2518	5	11/44	Surr 5/45, To UK, Fr *Roland Morillot* 1947, Str 1968
U.2519	5	11/44	Sc 5/45
U.2520	5	11/44	Sc 5/45
U.2521	5	11/44	Lost 5/5/45
U.2522	5	11/44	Sc 5/45
U.2523	5	12/44	Lost 17/1/45
U.2524	5	1/45	Lost 3/5/45
U.2525	5	12/44	Sc 5/45
U.2526	5	12/44	Sc 5/45
U.2527	5	12/44	Sc 5/45
U.2528	5	12/44	Sc 5/45
U.2529	5	1/45	Surr 5/45. To USSR as *N.27*, Str 1963
U.2530	5	12/44	Lost 11/3/45
U.2531	5	1/45	Sc 5/45
U.2532	5	—	Lost 31/12/44
U.2533	5	1/45	Sc 5/45
U.2534	5	1/45	Lost 6/5/45
U.2535	5	1/45	Sc 5/45
U.2536	5	1/45	Sc 5/45
U.2537	5	3/45	Lost 8/4/45
U.2538	5	2/45	Lost 9/5/45
U.2539	5	2/45	Sc 5/45
U.2540	5	2/45	Lost 3/5/45
U.2541	5	3/45	Sc 5/45
U.2542	5	3/45	Lost 3/4/45
U.2543	5	3/45	Sc 5/45
U.2544	5	3/45	Sc 5/45
U.2545	5	3/45	Sc 5/45
U.2546	5	4/45	Sc 5/45
U.2547	5	—	Lost 8/4/45
U.2548	5	3/45	Sc 5/45
U.2549-2550	5	—	Lost 8/4/45
U.2551	5	4/45	Sc 5/45
U.2552	5	4/45	Lost 8/4/45
U.2553-2564	5	—	BU incomplete
U.2565-2761	5	—	Canc
U.2762-3000	5	—	Projected
U.3001	3	7/44	Sc 5/45
U.3002	3	8/44	Sc 5/45
U.3003	3	8/44	Lost 4/4/45
U.3004	3	8/44	Sc 5/45
U.3005	3	9/44	Sc 5/45
U.3006	3	10/44	Sc 5/45
U.3007	3	10/44	Lost 24/2/45
U.3008	3	10/44	Su 5/45. To US, BU 1954
U.3009	3	11/44	Sc 5/45
U.3010	3	11/44	Sc 5/45
U.3011	3	12/44	Sc 5/45
U.3012	3	12/44	Sc 5/45
U.3013	3	11/44	Sc 5/45
U.3014	3	12/44	Sc 5/45
U.3015	3	12/44	Sc 5/45
U.3016	3	1/45	Sc 5/45
U.3017	3	1/45	Su 5/45. To UK as *N.41*, BU 1949
U.3018	3	1/45	Sc 5/45
U.3019	3	12/44	Sc 5/45
U.3020	3	12/44	Sc 5/45
U.3021	3	1/45	Sc 5/45
U.3022	3	1/45	Sc 5/45
U.3023	3	1/45	Sc 5/45
U.3024	3	1/45	Sc 5/45
U.3025	3	1/45	Sc 5/45
U.3026	3	1/45	Sc 5/45
U.3027	3	1/45	Sc 5/45
U.3028	3	1/45	Lost 3/5/45
U.3029	3	2/45	Sc 5/45
U.3030	3	2/45	Lost 3/5/45
U.3031	3	2/45	Sc 5/45
U.3032	3	2/45	Lost 3/5/45
U.3033	3	2/45	Sc 5/45
U.3034	3	3/45	Sc 5/45
U.3035	3	3/45	Su 5/45. To USSR as *N.28*, Str 1963
U.3036	3	2/45	Lost 4/45
U.3037	3	3/45	Sc 5/45
U.3038	3	3/45	Sc 5/45
U.3039	3	3/45	Sc 5/45
U.3040	3	3/45	Sc 5/45
U.3041	3	3/45	Surr 5/45. To USSR as *N.29*, Str 1963
U.3042-3043	3	—	Lost 4/45
U.3044	3	3/45	Sc 5/45
U.3045	3	—	BU incomplete
U.3046	3	—	BU incomplete
U.3047	3		Sc 5/45
U.3048	3		BU incomplete
U.3049	3		BU incomplete
U.3050	3		Sc 5/45
U.3051	3		Sc 5/45
U.3052-3061	3		BU incomplete
U.3062-3500	3	—	Projected
U.3501	50	7/44	Sc 5/45
U.3502	50	8/44	Sc 5/45
U.3503	50	9/44	Lost 5/5/45
U.3504	50	9/44	Sc 5/45
U.3505	50	10/44	Lost 3/5/45
U.3506	50	12/44	Sc 5/45
U.3507	50	10/44	Sc 5/45
U.3508	50	11/44	Lost 30/3/45
U.3509	50	11/44	Lost 9/44
U.3510	50	11/44	Sc 5/45
U.3511	50	11/44	Sc 5/45
U.3512	50	11/44	Lost 8/4/45
U.3513	50	12/44	Sc 5/45
U.3514	50	12/44	Surr 5/45†
U.3515	50	12/44	Surr 5/45. To USSR as *N.30*, Str 1963
U.3516	50	12/44	Sc 5/45
U.3517	50	12/44	SC 5/45
U.3518	50	12/44	Sc 5/45
U.3519	50	1/45	Lost 2/3/45
U.3520	50	1/45	Lost 31/1/45
U.3521	50	1/45	Sc 5/45
U.3522	50	1/45	Sc 5/45
U.3523	50	1/45	Lost 5/5/45
U.3524	50	1/45	Sc 5/45
U.3525	50	1/45	Sc 5/45
U.3526	50	3/45	Sc 5/45
U.3527	50	3/45	Sc 5/45
U.3528	50	2/45	Sc 5/45

U.3529	50	3/45	Sc 5/45
U.3530	50	3/45	Sc 5/45
U.3531-3537	50	—	BU 1946
U.3538-3542	50	—	Completed by USSR
U.3543-3695	50	—	BU or completed by USSR
U.3696-4000	50	—	Projected
U.4001-4120	21	—	BU incomplete
U.4121-4500	21	—	Projected
U.4501-4600	21	—	BU incomplete
U.4601-4700	21	—	Canc
U.4701	30	1/45	Sc 5/45
U.4702	30	1/45	Sc 5/45
U.4703	30	1/45	Sc 5/45
U.4704	30	3/45	Sc 5/45
U.4705	30	2/45	Sc 5/45
U.4706	30	2/45	Su 5/45. To UK, No as *Knerter* 1948, Str 1953
U.4707	30	2/45	Sc 5/45
U.4708	30	—	Lost 4/5/45
U.4709	30	3/45	Lost 4/5/45
U.4710	30	5/45	Sc 5/45
U.4711	30	3/45	Lost 4/5/45
U.4712	30	4/45	Lost 4/5/45
U.4713-4891	30	—	BU incomplete
U.4892-5000	30	—	Projected
U.5001-5003	33		Completed
U.5004-5100	30		Completed
U.5101-5250	30		Canc
U.5251-5350	51		Completed
U.5351-5750	51		Canc
U.5751-5800	37		Completed
U.5801-6170	37		Canc
U.6171-6200	37		Projected
U.6201-6245	30	—	BU incomplete
U.6246-6250	30	—	Canc
U.6251-6252	51		Completed
U.6253-6300	51	—	BU incomplete
U.6301-6351	51	—	Canc
UA	30	40	Sc 5/45
UB	14	11/40	Sc 5/45
UC.1	32	11/40	BU 1942
UC.2	32	11/40	Out of service 10/44
UD.1	8	11/40	Sc 3/5/45
UD.2	19	1/41	Out of service 7/44
UD.3	59	3/42	Sc 5/45
UD.4	48	3/41	Sc 5/45
UD.5	48	1/43	Surr 5/45 Returned to Ne as *0.27*, BU 1959
UF.1	16	—	Surr. Returned to Fr as *L'Africaine*, Str 1961
UF.2	16	11/42	Sc 5/45
UF.3	15	—	Surr. Returned to Fr as *L'Astrée*, Str 1965
UIT.1	45	9/43	Lost 4/9/44
UIT.2	45		Sc 4/45
UIT.3	45		Sc 4/45
UIT.4	12		Lost 20/4/44
UIT.5	12		Lost 20/4/44
UIT.6-9	12		Lost 16/3/45
UIT.10	12	—	Not completed
UIT.11	12	—	Not completed
UIT.12	12	—	Not completed
UIT.13	12	—	Not completed
UIT.14	12	—	Not completed
UIT.15	45		Lost 4/9/44
UIT.16	45		Lost 4/9/44
UIT.17	12		Sc 5/45
UIT.18	12		Sc 5/45
UIT.19	12		Lost 9/1/44. Yu *Sara* 1949
UIT.20	45		Lost 4/9/44
UIT.21	45		Sc 8/44
UIT.22	10		Lost 11/3/44
UIT.23	10		Lost 14/2/44
UIT.24	45		To Japan as *RO.503* qv
UIT.25	45		To Japan as *RO.504* qv

NOTE: Many submarines handed over to the UK, US and Canadian navies at the end of the war were never commissioned into those navies, but used for trials and experiments and subsequently sunk as targets or scrapped. Vessels noted as CTL were either scuttled or subsequently salvaged and scrapped.

†Scuttled in the North Atlantic during '*Operation Deadlight*' by the Allies in 1945-46.

ITALY

'H' Class: *H.1, H.2, H.4, H.6, H.8*

These submarines were built to a Holland design in Canada during World War I. They had originally been ordered for the Royal Navy as sister ships to the British 'H' class and Chilean Holland designs. The British order was subsequently completed for the Italian Navy. Following the end of the war the class was equipped with a 3inch gun, but the surviving vessels were obsolete by 1939. Like the British 'H' Class these boats were used for training during the war, proving particularly useful in working up new Italian corvettes engaged in A/S warfare.

'X' Class: *X.2, X.3*

These minelaying submarines were built during World War I, but the design was not successful. They had a very low surface speed and were not very manoeuvrable. The mines were laid from nine special tubes. Being obsolete by World War II both these vessels were laid up in 1940.

A Chilean submarine of the Fresia type, identical to the Italian 'H' class. *Courtesy Chilean Navy*

Balilla Class: ANTONIO SCIESA, BALILLA, DOMENICO MILLELIRE, ENRICO TOTI

This was the first class of submarine built by the Italian Navy after World War I. The design was based upon the German UEII cruising type. Realising the impracticability of mounting large calibre guns on submarines (such as the British, French and Americans had done) the Italians retained the standard 4.7inch gun. The concept of the cruising submarine was not, however, of any great value to the Italians, for the vessels were far too large to be of any practical use in the clear, constricted waters of the Mediterranean. Once the Italian East African Empire had crumbled there was no longer any need for cruiser-type submarines, for Italy did not pursue a submarine campaign thereafter in the Indian Ocean. These submarines were exceptionally well built, and were capable of diving to depths greater than any other submarine then afloat. The main machinery was placed much further forward than normal. The vessels were re-armed in 1934 with a 45-calibre 4.7inch gun. Another submarine of this class was built for the Brazilian Navy.

Antonio Sciesa in 1929. *Vicary*

Ballila in September 1930. Note the very large conning tower, a feature of many Italian submarines. *Wright & Logan*

Mameli Class: GIOVANNI DA PRODICA, GOFFREDO MAMELI (ex-*Masaniello*), PIER CAPPONI, TITO SPERI.

This class, like the previous cruiser-design, was very well constructed and capable of diving to great depths. The *Mameli* herself reached a depth of 64 fathoms (385 feet) on trials. The surviving vessels were re-engined in 1942 with new diesels developing 4,000 HP to increase the surfaced speed to 17 knots.

Pisani Class: DES GENEYS, GIOVANNI BAUSAN, MARCANTONIO COLONNA, VETTOR PISANI

This class, was very similar to the previous class but slightly larger. Like all pre-war Italian designs, however, they suffered from an enormous conning tower which resulted in poor stability. To overcome this the vessels had extra bulges fitted to the saddle tanks which reduced their surfaced speed from $17\frac{1}{4}$ knots to 15 knots.

Goffredo Mameli. This class was able to dive to great depths.
Courtesy Italian Navy

Vettor Pisani, very similar to the 'Mameli' class. They differed externally by having the gun mounted on a small platform with a breakwater. *Courtesy Italian Navy*

Ettore Fieramosca. Note that the conning tower, although still very large, has been to some extent streamlined to improve underwater performance. *Courtesy Italian Navy*

ETTORE FIERAMOSCA

This was the second design the Italians produced for a cruiser submarine. Only one vessel was ever completed to this design and she was used mainly as an experimental submarine. She was completed with a hangar and was to have carried a small seaplane; in the event, however, no aircraft was designed for this role and the hangar was finally removed in 1931. During the 1930's the vessel was regunned with a 45-calibre 4.7inch weapon.

Bragadin Class: MARCANTONIO BRAGADIN, FILIPPO CORRIDONI

This was the first class of minelaying submarine laid down for the Italian Navy after World War I. They were medium-sized boats, but the design was not a success. The boats were underpowered and the best surfaced speed did not exceed 11½ knots. As a consequence the design was not repeated and only two boats were completed. The mines were laid from two horizontal tubes.

Fillipo Corridoni. Courtesy Italian Navy

Bandiera Class: CIRO MENOTTI, FRATELLI BANDIERA, LUCIANO MANARA, SANTORRE SANTAROSA

This class resembled the earlier *Pisani* class, but were much larger, oceangoing vessels. Yet again the enormous conning tower, which in some cruiser-type submarines even included a small galley and WC (the Italians placed great emphasis on crew comfort) led to problems of instability. Bulges were added to the saddle tanks and the speed fell from 18/19 knots to 15/8¼ knots. The *Ciro Menotti* was re-armed in 1942 with a 47-calibre 3.9inch gun in place of the 4inch.

Fratelli Bandiera passing through the Suez Canal in January 1938. *Vicary*

Luigi Settembrini. Note that the raised bow has been dropped flush with the rest of the deck casing. *Courtesy Italian Navy*

Settembrini Class: LUIGI SETTEMBRINI, RUGGIERO SETTIMO

This class was very similar in many ways to the previous class. The conning tower was not quite so large, however, which improved stability somewhat, and the prominent hump in the deck casing at the bows was dispensed with. This greatly improved visibility at periscope depth and did much to reduce turbulence created in previous designs which had adopted the raised type of bow.

Squalo Class: DELFINO, NARVALO, SQUALO, TRICHECO

This class was basically a repeat of the earlier *Bandiera* class and as before suffered from instability.

Squalo. *Courtesy Italian Navy*

Argonauta Class: ARGONAUTA, FISALIA, JALEA, JANTINA, MEDUSA, SALPA, SERPENTE (ex-*Nautilus*)

At the time this was the largest class of submarines built by Italy since the end of World War I. The design for once proved successful and formed the basis for four subsequent designs which were almost identical. Together these classes were to form the backbone of Mussoloni's submarine Fleet designed to ensure that the Mediterranean was Italy's 'Mare Nostrum'.

Sirena Class: AMETISTA, ANFITRITE, DIAMANTE, GALATEA, NAIADE, NEREIDE, ONDINA, RUBINO, SIRENA, SMERALDO, TOPAZIO, ZAFFIRO

This was the first of the large class of submarines built to an almost identical design to the previous class. Like all Italian submarines they were completed with a large conning tower. Experience showed the weakness of the design and like most other submarines then afloat they were refitted with a smaller conning tower in 1942-43.

Nereide as completed with a large conning tower. *Courtesy Italian Navy*

PIETRO MICCA

This was another one-off design for a large submarine. She was the largest submarine built for the Italian Navy and was completed as a minelayer. As with other large Italian submarines the design was impractical for use in the Mediterranean. Performance was reasonable for such a large submarine, but her offensive capability was not outstanding, only 20 mines being carried. The British *Porpoise* Class of almost identical size carried a total of 50 mines.

Archimede Class: ARCHIMEDE (i), FERRARIS, GALILEI, TORRICELLI (i)

This was the first class of oceangoing submarines built for the Italian Navy to be armed with two guns. Previous designs had mounted only a single 4inch gun in front of the conning tower, but this class mounted two of the slightly lighter 3.9inch fore and aft of the conning tower. The nameship and *Toricelli* were transferred to Spain in 1937 as part of Italy's policy of assisting the Nationalist forces during the Civil War.

The *Pietro Micca* was the largest submarine built for the Italian Navy. *Courtesy Italian Navy*

Galilei. Courtesy Italian Navy

Calvi Class: ENRICO TAZZOLI, GIUSEPPE FINZI, PIETRO CALVI

These large cruiser-type submarines were an improved design of the earlier *Balilla* Class. They suffered from the same inherent disadvantages that all large submarines suffered in the Mediterranean. They were equipped with two extra stern torpedo tubes and an extra gun was carried abaft the conning tower. Both guns were bolted to the deck casing, as opposed to the partially shielded gun carried in an extension of the conning tower in the *Balilla* Class. In 1943 the *Enrico Tazzoli* and *Giuseppe Finzi* were converted to transport submarines for the carriage of raw materials from Japan. Italy surrendered before the conversion of *Giuseppe Finzi* was complete and she was taken over by the Germans.

Perla Class: AMBRA, BERILLO, CORALLO, DIASPRO, GEMMA, IRIDE (ex-*Iris*), MALACHITE, ONICE, PERLA, TURCHESE

This was the second largest class of submarines built to a design almost identical to that of the *Argonauta* class. Dimensions were the same as the *Sirena* class, and although more powerful diesels were fitted, surfaced speed remaining the same. During 1937 the *Iride* and *Onice* were loaned to the Nationalist forces in Spain for the duration of the Civil War.

Foca Class: ATROPO, FOCA, ZOEA

These three submarines were the last to be purpose-built as minelayers for the Italian Navy. They were equipped with two minelaying chutes for the discharge of the 36 mines carried. As built the 3.9inch gun was fitted in a turret mount on a rear extension of the conning tower. This was subsequently removed and the conning tower reduced in size, for reasons stated above, and a 47-calibre 3.9inch gun fitted on the foredeck casing.

Foca, one of the last purpose built minelayers, is shown as first completed. *Courtesy Italian Navy*

Adua Class: ADUA, ALAGI, ARADAM, ASCIANGHI (i), ASCIANGHI (ii), AXUM, BEILUL, DAGABUR, DESSIÉ, DURBO, GONDAR (i), GONDAR (ii), LAFOLÉ, MACALLÉ, NEGHELLI (i), NEGHELLI (ii), SCIRÉ, TEMBIEN UARSCIEK, UEBI SCEBELI

This class was the third built to a design almost identical to the *Argonauta*. The first *Ascianghi*, *Gondar* and *Neghelli* were transferred to Brazil in September 1937 when they were completed. During 1941 the *Gondar* (ii) and *Sciré* had the 3.9inch gun removed and three cylinders fitted to the deck casing fore and aft of the conning tower for the transport of human torpedoes.

SLC — 'MAIALE'

These piloted 'torpedoes' were developed from similar weapons devised for attacking protected Austrian harbours during World War I. The weapon was basically a miniature submarine with electric propulsion and joystick steering control. It was manned by two divers wearing frogmen suits and long-range underwater breathing apparatus. In addition to a detachable explosive warhead sufficient tools were carried in lockers for the divers to deal with many kinds of underwater obstacles, including A/S nets. Initial models of the weapon were built early in 1936. At first it was planned to transport the weapons clamped to chocks on the decks of submarines, but the weapon was not resistant to pressures below 16 fathoms and so this made the submarine vulnerable. A new means of transportation was therefore devised, which consisted of pressure-resistant watertight cylinders welded to the decks of the parent submarines; three in the seagoing classes (one fore and two side aft of the conning tower) and four in the oceangoing classes (two side by side fore and aft of the conning tower).

Brin Class: ARCHIMEDE, BRIN, GALVANI, GUGLIELMOTTI, TORRICELLI

These vessels were almost identical to the previous oceangoing *Archimede* Class. The *Archimede* and *Toricelli* of this class were in fact built in complete secrecy to replace the two vessels of the *Archimede* Class transferred to Spanish Nationalist forces in 1937 (see above). When first completed this class carried the 3.9inch gun in a trainable turret mount as in the *Foca* Class. These were subsequently replaced by a 47-calibre 3.9inch gun mounted on the foredeck casing.

A 'Brin' class submarine as first completed. *Courtesy Italian Navy*

Marcello Class: BARBARIGO, DANDOLO, EMO, MARCELLO, MOCENIGO, MOROSINI, NANI, PROVANA, VENIERO

This class was fitted with an extremely large conning tower equipped with many refinements, including a galley and WC for the watch-keepers. As with other classes these vessels suffered from instability. The gun arrangement was the same as in the *Archimede* Class, while internally two extra reload torpedoes were carried. The *Barbarigo* was converted to a transport submarine early in 1943.

Agostino Barbarigo in 1943. *M. Bar*

Comandante Cappellini. *Courtesy Italian Navy*

Midget submarine *CA.1* as rebuilt. *Courtesy Italian Navy*

Cappellini Class: COMANDANTE CAPPELLINI, COMMANDANTE FAA DI BRUNO

This class was a virtual repeat of the previous class. The *Comandante Cappellini* was converted to a transport submarine during 1943. When Italy surrendered she was taken over at Sabang by the Japanese who handed her over to the Germans who re-armed her with a single 4.1inch gun.

'CA' Class: Group I-*CA.1*, *CA.2* Group II*-*CA.3*, *CA.4*

These midget submarines were originally designed for use in the Adriatic and Black Sea areas. The design was based upon the midget submarines built during World War I, but displacement was reduced to a minimum in order that the midgets could be transported on the decks of large submarines. The limited range and advanced A/S tactics rendered the value of the CA Class midgets problematical and with the success of the 'Maiale' (Pigs) it was decided to rebuild the midgets for other special duties. The first group was rebuilt during 1941-42 and plans were drawn up for them to be used to attack harbours on the American East Coast. To this end the *Leonardo da Vinci* stationed under BETASOM at Bordeaux was equipped to carry one of these small midgets. *CA.2* was transported to Bordeaux, but the *Leonardo da Vinci* was sunk before the plan could be put into operation.

Midget submarine *CA.2* as rebuilt. *Courtesy Italian Navy*

Marconi. *Courtesy Italian Navy*

Marconi Class: ALESSANDRO MALASPINA, GUGLIELMO MARCONI, LEONARDO DA VINCI, LUIGI TORELLI, MAGGIORE BARACCA, MICHELE BIANCHI

The *Marconi* class oceangoing submarines had a much greater radius of action than earlier oceangoing types. The increased bunkerage necessary was achieved at the expense of offensive capability, however, and only four reload torpedoes were carried as opposed to eight in earlier oceangoing vessels. During 1943 the *Luigi Torelli* was converted to a transport submarine for the carriage of raw materials from the Far East. She was at Singapore on her first such trip when Italy surrendered and the Japanese seized the submarine and handed her over to the Germans.

Liuzzi Class: ALPINO BAGNOLINI, CAPITANO TARANTINI, CONSOLE GENERALE LIUZZI, REGINALDO GIULIANI

These oceangoing submarines were a virtual repeat of the *Marconi* Class. During 1943 the *Alpino Bagnolini* and *Reginaldo Giuliani* were converted to transport submarines. When Italy surrendered in September 1943 *Alpino Bagnolini* was still at Bordeaux while the *Reginaldo Giuliani* had reached Singapore on her first trip to the Far East to pick up a cargo of raw material.

Console Generale Liuzzi. *Courtesy Italian Navy*

Acciaio Class: ACCIAIO, ALABASTRO, ARGENTO*. ASTERIA, AVORIO, BRONZO*, COBALTO, GIADA, GRANITO, NICHELIO, PLATINO, PROFIDO, VOLFRAMIO (ex-*Stronzio*)*

This was the fourth and last class of almost identical design to the *Argonauta* Class. More powerful diesels were fitted but with increased displacement overall performance remained the same.

Submarine of the 'Acciaio' Class. *Real Photos*

Granito in dry dock in 1942. *Author's Collection*

Cagni Class: AMMIRAGLIO CAGNI, AMMIRAGLIO CARACCIOLO, AMMIRAGLIO MILLO, AMMIRAGLIO SAINT-BON

This was the last class of cruiser-submarines built for the Italian Navy and they were specifically designed as commerce raiders. For this they departed from normal practice and were fitted with much smaller torpedo tubes enabling a larger number to be carried. In addition the smaller torpedoes permitted a much larger number of reloads to be carried. These vessels were capable of remaining on patrol unsupported for a very long time. During 1943 the *Ammiraglio Cagni* was converted to a transport submarine.

'CB' Class: *CB.1-72*

This class of midget submarines was developed from the earlier 'CA' type and were employed in a normal submarine role in the Black Sea and Adriatic. Displacement and dimensions were increased and a standard diesel/electric propulsion fitted. They were better constructed and much more seaworthy than the earlier 'CA' type.

Midget submarines of the 'CB' type at Sevastopol in October 1942. *Courtesy Italian Navy*

Ammiraglio Saint Bon. Courtesy Italian Navy

Flutto Classs: Group I — CERNIA, DENTICE, FLUTTO, GORGO, GRONGO, MAREA, MURENA, NAUTILO, SPARIDE, SPIGOLA, TRITONE, VORTICE Group II* — ALLUMINIO, AMIANTO, ANTIMONIO, BARIO, CADMIO, CROMO, FERRO, FOSFORO, IRIDIO, LITIO, MAGNESIO, MANGANESE, MERCURIO, ORO, OTTONE, PIOMBO, POTASSIO, RAME, RUTENIO, SILICIO, SODIO, VANADIO, ZINCO, ZOLFO Group III*. — ATTINIO, AZOTO, BROMO, CARBONIO, ELIO, MOLIBDENO, OSMIO, OSSIGENO, PLUTONIO, RADIO, SELENIO, TUNGSTENO

This was the last class of seagoing submarines to be built for the Italian Navy. They were a slightly enlarged edition of the previous seagoing designs which had proved so successful. More powerful diesels were fitted giving an extra 2 knots surfaced speed and four extra reload torpedoes were carried. *Grongo* and *Murena* were fitted with two watertight cylinders on the saddle tanks amidships for the transport of SLC. Large numbers of this class were planned, but owing to Italy's surrender were never completed or laid down. The names assigned to the Group III vessels (ordered in the Spring and Summer of 1943) are not verified.

Marea (first group). *Author's Collection*

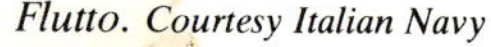

Flutto. Courtesy Italian Navy

'R' Class: REMO, ROMOLO, *R.3-12*

The desperate shortage of raw materials necessary for war production led to the design of this class of transport submarines. They were designed to carry cargo from the Far East and so carried a greatly reduced armament and had extensive bunkerage. Only two of the class were completed before Italy surrendered.

'CM' Class: *CM.1-19*

This class of small coastal submarines was developed for harbour defence purposes following the bombardment and mining of Italian ports by the British Mediterranean Fleet. The old submarines of the 'H' Class were totally unsuitable for such operations by late 1942 when the 'CM' Class was designed.

Romolo after launching on March 21, 1943. *Courtesy Italian Navy*

CM.1. *Courtesy Italian Navy*

Argo. *Courtesy Italian Navy*

Glauco. Courtesy Italian Navy

'CC' Class: *CC.1-3, C.23-56*

This class was almost identical to the preceeding 'CM' class.

FOREIGN SUBMARINES

Ex-Portuguese *Argo* Class: ARGO, VELELLA

These two submarines, originally ordered by Portugal in 1931, were incorporated into the Italian Navy in 1935 when for economic reasons Portugal cancelled the order.

Ex-Portuguese: GLAUCO (ex-*Delfim*), OTARIA (ex-*Espadarte*)

Like the two previous submarines these vessels were ordered by Portugal in 1931 but construction ceased a few days after being laid down when the order was cancelled. The vessels were subsequently completed for the Italian Navy.

Ex-German Type VIIc: *S.1* (ex-*U.428*), *S.2* (ex-*U.746*), *S.3* (ex-*U.747*), *S.4* (ex-*U.429*), *S.5* (ex-*U.748*), *S.6* (ex-*U.430*), *S.7* (ex-*U.749*), *S.8* (ex-*U.1161*), *S.9* (ex-*U.750*)
Ex-Yugoslav: *ANTONIO BAJAMONTI* (ex-*SMELI*), *FRANCESCO RISMONDO* (ex-*OSVETNIK*)
Ex-Yugoslav: *N.3* (ex-*HRABRI*)
Ex-French *Requin* Class: *FR.111* (ex-*PHOQUE*), *FR.113* (ex-*REQUIN*), *FR.114* (ex-*ESPADON*), *FR.115* (ex-*DAUPHIN*)
Ex-French *Saphir* Class: *FR.112* (ex-*SAPHIR*), *FR.116* (ex-*TURQUOISE*), (ex-*NAUTILUS*)
Ex-French *Sirène* Class: *FR.117* (ex-*CIRCÉ*), (ex-*CALYPSO*)
Ex-French *Archimède* Class: *FR.119* (ex-*HENRI POINCARÉ*)

CLASS	'SLC'	'CA'	'CB'
TYPE	Human Torpedo	Midget	Midget
DISPLACEMENT		13½(12†,12¾*)/16½(14†*)	25/45
DIMENSIONS			
METRIC	6.7×.5	10(10.5*)×1.96(1.9*)×1.6(1.8*)	15×3×2
IMPERIAL	22×1½	32½(39¼*)×6½(6¼*)×5¼(6*)	49×9¾×6½
MACHINERY			
HP	1	60/25	50/80
SPEED	4½	6¼(7†*)/5(6†*)	7½/7
RADIUS	4/15		
SPEED	4½/2¼		
FUEL			
DIVING LIMIT	16		
ARMAMENT			
GUNS	—	—	—
TORPEDO TUBES	—	—	—
SITING	—	—	—
NO OF TORPEDOES/		2×450(17.7)(removed 1941)	2×450 (17.7) or
MINES	300Kg detachable warhead	8×100kg charges (+20×2Kg in*)	2M
COMPLEMENT	2	2 (3†*)	4

†as rebuilt 1941

CLASS	*MAMELI*	*PISANI*	*ARGONAUTA*	*SIRENA*	*PERLA*	*ADUA*
TYPE	Seagoing	Seagoing	Seagoing	Seagoing	Seagoing	Seagoing
DISPLACEMENT	786/1,009	807/1,057	611/810	623/860	626/860	623/866
DIMENSIONS						
METRIC	64.6×6.5×4.3	68.2×6.1×4.9	61.5×5.7×4.7	60.2×6.45×4.7	60.2×6.45×4.7	60.2×6.45×4.7
IMPERIAL	212×22¼×14	223×20×16	200×18¾×15½	197½×21¼×13½	197½×21¼×15½	197½×21¼×15½
MACHINERY						
HP	3,1000/1,100	3,000/1,100	1,200/800	1,200/800	1,400/800	1,200/800
SPEED	15/7¼	17¼/8¼	14/8	14/7¾	14/7½	14/7½
RADIUS	3,500/65	5,000/108	4,000/80	4,000/80	4,000/80	4,000/80
SPEED	8/4	8/4	9/8	9/8	9/8	9/8
FUEL	70	70				
DIVING LIMIT	55				50	
ARMAMENT						
GUNS	1×102/35(4) 2×13.2	1×102/35(4) 2×13.2	1×102/35(4) 2×13.2	1×100/47(3.9) 2-4×13.2	1×100/47(3.9) 2-4×13.2	1×100/47(3.9) 2-4×13.2
TORPEDO TUBES	6×533(21)	6×533(21)	6×533(21)	6×533(21)	6×533(21)	6×533(21)
SITING	4 bow 2 stern	4 bow 2 stern	6 bow	6 bow	4 bow 2 stern	6 bow
NO OF TORPEDOES/ MINES	10	9	12	12	12	12
COMPLEMENT	49	49	44	45	45	45

CLASS	*ACCIAIO*	*FLUTTO*	*'H'*	*'CM'*	*'CC'*
TYPE	Seagoing	Seagoing	Coastal	Coastal	Coastal
DISPLACEMENT	643/871	750(766*)/1,068(1,131*)	342/441	92/114	99½/117
DIMENSIONS					
METRIC	60.18×6.45×4.7	63.15(64.19*)×6.98×4.87(4.93*)	44.5×4.7×3.8	33×2.9×2.7	33×2.7×2.2
IMPERIAL	197½×21¼×15½	207¼(210¾*)×23×16(16¼*)	146×15½×12½	108×9½×9	108×8¾×7¼
MACHINERY					
HP	1,400(1,500*)/800	2,400/800	620/448	660/120	700/120
SPEED	14(14¾*)/7¾	16/8½(8*)	12/11	14/8	16/9
RADIUS		5,400/80	1,350/130		
SPEED		8/4	12/2		
FUEL			16		
DIVING LIMIT			27		
ARMAMENT					
GUNS	1×100/47(3.9) 1-2×20, 2-4×13.2	1×100/47(3.9) 2×20, 2-4×13.2	1×75/30(3)	2×13.2 (not mounted)	2×13.2
TORPEDO TUBES	6(4*)×533 (21)	6×533 (21)	4×450(17.7)	3×450(17.7)	3×450(17.7)
SITING		4 bow 2 stern	4 bow		
NO OF TORPEDOES/ MINES	8	12	6	3	3
COMPLEMENT	50	54	27	8	8

CLASS	*BANDIERA*	*SETTEMBRINI*	*SQUALO*	*ARCHIMEDE*	*BRIN*
TYPE	Oceangoing	Oceangoing	Oceangoing	Oceangoing	Oceangoing
DISPLACEMENT	866/1,153	872/1,153	857/1,142	880/1,259	913/1,266
DIMENSIONS					
METRIC	69.8×7.3×5.26	69.1×6.6×4.45	69.8×7.2×5.2	70.5×6.87×4.1	70.5×6.7×4.5
IMPERIAL	229×24×17¼	228×21½×14½	229×23¾×17	231¼×22½×13½	231¼×22×14¾

CLASS	*BANDIERA*	*SETTEMBRINI*	*SQUALO*	*ARCHIMEDE*	*BRIN*
MACHINERY					
HP	3,000/1,300	3,000/1,400	3,000/1,300	3,000/1,100	3,400/1,300
SPEED	18/9	17½/7¾	17/8½	17/7¾	17⅓/8
RADIUS	9,000/80	9,000/80	8,500/72	10,500/105	
SPEED	8/4	8/4	8/4	8/3	
FUEL				100	
DIVING LIMIT			58		60
ARMAMENT					
GUNS	1×102/35(4) 2×13.2	1×102/35(4) 4×13.2	1×102/35(4) 2×13.2	2×100/43(3.9) 2×13.2	1×100/43(3.9) 4×13.2
TORPEDO TUBES	8×533(21)	8×533(21)	8×533(21)	8×533(21)	8×533(21)
SITING	4 bow 4 stern	4 bow 4 stern	4 bow 4 stern	4 bow 4 stern	4 bow 4 stern
NO OF TORPEDOES/ MINES	12	12	12	16	14
COMPLEMENT	52	56	54	55	59

CLASS	*MARCELLO*	*CAPPELLINI*	*MARCONI*	*LIUZZI*
TYPE	Oceangoing	Oceangoing	Oceangoing	Oceangoing
DISPLACEMENT	962/1,317	955/1,313	1,036/1,489	1,031/1,484
DIMENSIONS				
METRIC	73×7.2×5	73×7.2×5	76.5×6.8×4.7	76.1×6.98×4.5
IMPERIAL	239½×23¾×16¾	239½×23¾×16¾	250×22¼×15½	249¾×23×14¾
MACHINERY				
HP	3,000/1,100	3,600/1,100	3,600/1,500	3,500/1,500
SPEED	17½/8	17½/8	18/8	18/8
RADIUS	7,500/80	7,500/120	10,500/110	9,500/80
SPEED	9/4	9/3	8/3	9/4
FUEL			200	
DIVING LIMIT	58	70	65	
ARMAMENT				
GUNS	2×100/47(3.9) 4×13.2	2×100/47(3.9) 4×13.2	1×100/47(3.9) 4×13.2	1×100/47(3.9) 4×13.2
TORPEDO TUBES	8×533 (21)	8×533 (21)	8×533 (21)	8×533 (21)
SITING	4 bow 4 stern	4 bow 4 stern	4 bow 4 stern	4 bow 4 stern
NO OF TORPEDOES/ MINES	16	16	12	12
COMPLEMENT	58	58	57	58

CLASS	*BALILLA*	*FIERAMOSCA*	*CALVI*	*CAGNI*
TYPE	Cruiser	Cruiser	Cruiser	Cruiser
DISPLACEMENT	1,368/1,904	1,400/2,128	1,331/2,060	1,504/2,170
DIMENSIONS				
METRIC	86.75×7.8×4.7	84×8.3×5	84.3×7.7×5.2	87.9×7.76×5.7
IMPERIAL	284×25½×15½	275½×27¼×16½	276¾×25¼×17	288×25½×18¾
MACHINERY				
HP	4,900/2,200 + 425	5,200/2,000	4,400/1,800	4,370/1,800
SPEED	17½/8¾ 7	19/10	17/8	17/8½
RADIUS	13,000/80	5,000/80	13,500/80	
SPEED	9/4	9/4	9/4	
FUEL	140	150		
DIVING LIMIT	67		55	

CLASS	BALILLA	FIERAMOSCA	CALVI	CAGNI
ARMAMENT				
GUNS	1×120/27(4.7) 4×13.2	1×120/27(4.7) 4×13.2	2×120/45(4.7) 4×13.2	2×100/47(3.9) 4×13.2
TORPEDO TUBES	6×533(21)	8×533(21)	8×533(21)	14×450(17.7)
SITING	4 bow 2 stern		4 bow 4 stern	
NO OF TORPEDOES/ MINES	16+4M (only in Balilla)	14	16	36
COMPLEMENT	78	78	78	85

CLASS	X.2	BRAGADIN	MICCA	FOCA
TYPE	Minelayer	Minelayer	Minelayer	Minelayer
DISPLACEMENT	394/468	833/1,085	1,371/1,970	1,215/1,659
DIMENSIONS				
METRIC	42.6×5.5×3.2	71.5×6.15×5	90.3×7.7×5.3	82.85×7.17×5.3
IMPERIAL	140×18×3	234½×22×16¼	295×25¼×17¼	272×24½×17¼
MACHINERY				
HP	650/325	1,500/1,000	3,000/1,500	2,880/1,250
SPEED	8¼/6⅓	11½/7	15½/8½	16/8
RADIUS	1,360/96	9,000/72	12,000/80	8,550/106
SPEED	6½/4	8/4	8/4	8/4
FUEL	18			
DIVING LIMIT				58
ARMAMENT				
GUNS	1×76 130(3)	1×102/35(4) 2×13.2	2×120/45(4.7) 4×13.2	1×100/43(3.9) 4×13.2
TORPEDO TUBES	2×450 (17.7)	4×533 (21)	6×533 (21)	6×533 (21)
SITING	2 bow	4 bow	6 bow	6 bow
NO OF TORPEDOES/ MINES	2+18M	6+16/24M	10+20M	8+36M
COMPLEMENT	25	55	72	60

Name	Builder	In Service	Fate
Acciaio	45	1/42	Lost 13/7/43
Adua	12	11/36	Lost 30/9/41
Alabastro	12	5/42	Lost 14/9/42
Alagi	12	2/37	BU 1947
Alessandro Malaspina	12	6/40	Lost 9/41
Alluminio	12	—	Seized 9/43. (Ger). Str
Alpino Bagnolini	10	12/39	Seized 9/43. (Ger.*UIT.22*) qv
Ambra	45	8/36	Sc 9/43
Ametista	45	4/34	Sc 9/43
Amianto	10	—	Canc
Ammiraglio Cagni	12	4/41	Str 1948
Ammiraglio Caracciolo	12	6/41	Lost 11/12/41
Ammiraglio Millo	12	5/41	Lost 14/3/42
Ammiraglio Saint-Bon	12		Lost 5/1/42
Anfitrite	12	3/34	Lost 6/3/41
Antimonio	45	—	Seized 9/43. (Ger). Str
Antonio Bajamonti	14	4/41	Sc 9/43
Antonio Sciesa	45	4/29	Sc 11/42
Aradam	12	1/37	Sc 9/43. CTL
Archimede (i)	10	4/37	Trf Spain (*Gen.Sanjurjo*)
Archimede (ii)	10	4/39	Lost 15/4/43
Argento	10	5/42	Lost 3/8/43
Argo	12	8/37	Sc 9/43
Argonauta	12	1/32	Lost 28/6/40
Ascianghi (i)	45	9/37	Trf Brazil (*Tamoyo*)
Ascianghi (ii)	45	3/38	Lost 23/7/43
Asteria	12	11/41	Lost 17/2/43
Atropo	10	2/39	Str 1947
Attinio		—	Canc
Avorio	12	3/42	Lost 9/2/43
Axum	12	12/38	MC 28/12/43
Azoto		—	Canc
Balilla	45	7/28	Str 1946
Barbarigo	12	9/38	Lost 19/6/43
Bario	12	—	Seized 9/43 Ger *UIT.7* qv
Beilul	45	9/38	Seized 9/43 (Ger). Lost 5/44
Berillo	12	8/36	Lost 2/10/40
Brin	10	6/38	Str 1948
Bromo		—	Canc
Bronzo	10	1/42	Captured 12/7/43 (UK *P.714*)
CA.1	13	4/38	Sc 9/43
CA.2	13	4/38	Sc 1944
CA.3	13	1/43	Sc 9/43

Name	Builder	In Service	Fate
CA,4	13	1/43	Sc 9/43
Cadmio	12	—	Canc
Capitano Tarantini	10	3/40	Lost 15/12/40
Carbonio		—	Canc
CB.1-2	13	1/41	Trf Ro 9/43 qv
CB.3-4	13	5/41	Trf Ro 9/43 qv
CB.5	13	5/41	Lost 13/6/42
CB.6	13	5/41	Trf Ro 9/43 qv
CB.7	13	8/43	Seized 9/43. (Ger)
CB.8-12	13	8/43	Str 1948
CB13-22	13		Seized 9/43 (Ger)
CB.23-36	13	—	Canc
CC.1	13	—	Str 1945
CC.2-3	13	—	Canc
CC.23-56	13	—	Canc
Cernia	10	—	Canc, BU
Ciro Menotti	45	8/30	Str 1948
CM.1	12	—	Seized 9/43 (Ger.*UIT.17*) qv
CM.2	12	—	Seized 9/43 (Ger.*UIT.18*) qv
CM.3-19	12	—	Canc
Cobalto	45	1/42	Lost 12/8/42
Comandante Cappellini	45	9/39	Seized 9/43 (Ger.*UIT.24*) qv
Comandante Faà di Bruno	45	10/39	Lost /11/40
Console Generale Liuzzi	10	11/39	Lost 27/6/40
Corallo	12	9/36	Lost 13/12/42
Cromo	12	—	Seized 9/43. (Ger). Str
Dagabur	10	4/37	Lost 12/8/42
Dandolo	12	3/38	Str 1948
Delfino	12	6/31	MC 23/3/43
Dentice	10	—	Canc. Str
Des Geneys	9	10/29	Str 1946
Dessiè	10	4/37	Lost 28/11/42
Diamante	10	11/33	Lost 20/6/40
Diaspro	12	8/36	Str 1948
Domenico Millelire	45	8/28	Str 1946
Durbo	45	7/38	Lost 18/10/40
Elio		—	Canc
Emo	12	10/38	Lost 10/11/42
Enrico Tazzoli	45	4/36	Lost 5/43
Enrico Toti	45	9/28	Str 1946
Ettore Fieramosca	10	4/30	Str 1946
Ferraris	10	1/35	Lost 25/10/41
Ferro	12	—	Seized 9/43 (Ger.*UIT.12*) qv
Filippo Corridoni	10	11/31	Str 1948
Fisalia	12	6/32	Lost 28/9/41
Flutto	12	3/43	Lost 11/7/43
Foca	10	11/37	Lost 13/10/40
Fosforo	45	—	Seized 9/43. (Ger). Str
FR.111	7	1/43	Lost 28/2/43
FR.112	56	—	Str 4/43
FR.113	17	—	Sc 9/43. CTL
FR.114	56	—	Sc 9/43
FR.115		—	Sc 9/43
FR.116	56	—	Sc 6/5/43
FR.117	52	—	Sc 5/43
FR.118	39	—	Seized 9/43. (Ger). Str
Francesco Rismondo	4	4/41	Seized 9/43. (Ger). Sc 9/43
Fratelli Bandiera	9	9/30	Str 1948
Galatea	12	6/34	Str 1948
Galilei	10	10/34	Captured 19/6/40 (UK *X.2*)
Galvani	10	7/38	Lost 24/6/40
Gemma	12	7/36	MC 8/10/40
Giada	12	12/41	Str 1966
Giovanni Bausan	9	9/29	Str 1946
Giovanni da Procida	10	1/29	Str 1948
Giuseppe Finzi	45	1/36	Seized 9/43 (Ger.*UIT.21*) qv
Glauco	12	9/35	Lost 27/6/41
Goffredo Mameli	10	1/29	Str 1948
Gondar (i)	45	9/37	Trf Brazil 9/37 (*Timbyra*)
Gondar (ii)	45	2/38	Lost 30/9/40
Gorgo	12	11/42	Lost 21/5/43
Granito	12	1/42	Lost 9/11/42
Grongo	45	—	Seized 9/43 (Ger.*UIT.20*) qv
Guglielmo Marconi	12	2/40	Lost 11/41
Guglielmotti	10	10/38	Lost 17/3/42
H.1-2	8	12/16	Str 1947
H.4	8	5/17	Str 1947
H.6	8	7/17	Seized 9/43. (Ger). Sc
H.8	8	6/18	Lost 5/6/43
Iride	45	11/36	Lost 22/8/40
Iridio	12	—	Canc
Jalea	45	3/33	Str 1948
Jantina	45	3/33	Lost 5/7/41
Lafolè	45	8/38	Lost 20/10/40
Leonardo da Vinci	12	4/40	Lost 23/5/43
Litio	12	—	Seized 9/43 (Ger.*UIT.8*) qv
Luciano Manara	9	6/30	Str 1948
Luigi Settembrini	10	1/32	MC 15/11/44
Luigi Torelli	45	5/40	Seized 9/43. (Ger.*UIT.25*) qv
Macallé	45	3/37	MC 15/6/40
Maggiore Baracca	45	7/40	Lost 8/9/41
Magnesio	10	—	Canc
Malachite	45	11/36	Lost 9/2/43
Manganese	45	—	Seized 9/43. (Ger). Str
Marcantonio Bragadin	10	11/31	Str 1948
Marcantonio Colonna	9	7/29	Str 1943
Marcello	12	3/38	Lost 22/2/41
Marea	12	5/43	Trf USSR 2/49. Str 1960
Medusa	12	9/32	Lost 30/1/42
Mercurio	10	—	Canc
Michele Bianchi	45	4/40	Lost 7/8/41
Molibdeno		—	Canc
Morosini	12	11/38	Lost 11/8/42
Murena	45	8/43	Sc 9/43. Seized (Ger.*UIT.16*) qv
N.3	57	4/41	Str 1941
Naiade	12	11/33	Lost 14/12/40
Nani	12	9/38	Lost 7/1/41
Narvalo	12	12/30	Lost 14/1/43
Nautilo	12	7/43	Sc 9/43. Seized (Ger.*UIT.19*) qv
Neghelli (i)	45	9/37	Trf Brazil 1937 (*Tupy*)
Neghelli (ii)	45	2/38	Lost 19/1/41
Nereide	12	2/34	Lost 13/7/43
Nichelio	45	7/42	Trf USSR 2/49. Str 1960
Ondina	12	9/34	Lost 11/7/42
Onice	45	9/36	Str 1947
Oro	12	—	Canc
Osmio		—	Canc
Ossigeno		—	Canc
Otaria	12	10/35	Str 1948
Ottone	12	—	Canc

Perla	12	7/36	Captured 9/7/42. (UK.*P.712*)
Pier Capponi	10	1/29	Lost 31/3/41
Pietro Calvi	45	10/35	Lost 15/7/42
Pietro Micca	10	10/35	Lost 29/7/43
Piombo	12	—	Seized 9/43. (Ger.*UIT.13*) qv
Platino	45	10/41	Str 1948
Plutonio		—	Canc
Porfido	12	1/42	Lost 6/12/42
Potassio	12	—	Seized 9/43 (Ger.*UIT.10*) qv
Provana	12	6/38	Lost 17/6/40
R.3-6	10	—	Str
R.7-9	12	—	Seized 9/43. (Ger.*UIT.4-6*) qv
R.10-12	45	—	Seized 9/43. (Ger.*UIT.1-3*) qv
Radio		—	Canc
Rame	12	—	Seized 9/43. (Ger.*UIT.11*) qv
Reginaldo Giuliani	10	2/40	Seized 9/43. (Ger.*UIT.23*) qv
Remo	10	6/43	Lost 15/7/43
Romolo	10	6/43	Lost 18/7/43
Rubino	11	3/34	Lost 29/6/40
Ruggiero Settimo	10	4/32	Str 1948
Rutenio	12	—	Canc
S.1	18	6/43	Ger 9/43 (*U.428*) qv
S.2-3	50	7/43	Ger 9/43 (*U.746-747*) qv
S.4	18	7/43	Ger 9/43 (*U.429*) qv
S.5	50	7/43	Ger 9/43 (*U.748*) qv
S.6	18	8/43	Ger 9/43 (*U.430*) qv
S.7	50	8/43	Ger 9/43 (*U.749*) qv
S.8	18	8/43	Ger 9/43 (*U.1161*) qv
S.9	50	8/43	Ger 9/43 (*U.750*) qv
Salpa	10	12/32	Lost 27/6/41
Santorre Santarosa	45	7/30	Lost 20/1/43
Sciré	45	3/38	Lost 10/8/42
Selenio		—	Canc
Serpente	10	11/32	Sc 9/43
Silicio	45	—	Seized 9/43 (Ger). Str 1943
Sirena	12	10/33	Sc 9/43
Smeraldo	10	11/33	Lost 16/9/41
Sodio	12	—	Seized 9/43 (Ger.*UIT.9*) qv
Sparide	45	8/43	Sc 9/43. Seized (Ger.*UIT.15*) qv
Spigola	10	—	Canc 1943. BU 1948
Squalo	12	10/30	Str 1948
Tembien	45	7/38	Lost 2/8/41
Tito Speri	10	8/29	Str 1948
Topazio	11	4/34	MC 12/9/43
Toricelli (i)	10	4/37	Trf Spain (*Gen.Mola*)
Toricelli (ii)	10	5/39	Lost 23/6/40
Tricheco	12	6/31	Lost 18/3/42
Tritone	12	10/42	Lost 19/1/43
Tungsteno		—	Canc
Turchese	12	9/36	Str 1948
Uarsciek	10	12/37	Lost 15/12/42
Uebi Scebeli	10	12/37	Lost 29/6/40
Vanadio	12	—	Canc
Velella	12	9/37	Lost 7/9/43
Veniero	12	6/38	Lost 7/6/42
Vettor Pisani	9	6/29	Str 1948
Volframio	10	2/42	Sc 9/43. CTL
Vortice	12	6/43	Str 1967
Zaffiro	45	6/34	Lost 9/6/42
Zinco	12	—	Seized 9/43 (Ger.*UIT.14*) qv
Zoea	10	2/38	Str 1947
Zolfo	45	—	Seized 9/43 (Ger). Str 1943

JAPAN

Type L1: *RO.51-52* (ex-Nos. *25-26*) L2*: *RO.53-56* (ex-*Nos. 27-30*) L3†: *RO.57-59* (ex-*Nos.46-47, 57*)

These designs were based upon plans of the 'L' Class supplied by Britain and executed in Japan. The Type L1 vessels carried two broadside torpedo tubes amidships but these were removed in the later vessels. Dimensions and displacement were slightly increased in the Type L3, but in other respects the design remained the same. As in the British 'L' Class the gun was mounted in the conning tower. By the outbreak of war these submarines were obsolete and those not withdrawn from service were employed in training new submarine crews.

Type KD1: *I.51* (ex-*No.44*)

The design of this submarine was based upon the fleet type submarines built for the Royal Navy towards the close of World War I. Initially the vessel was completed with four shafts driven by four diesels. This system did not prove very successful and not long after completion two of the shafts and their associated diesels were removed. The 3-inch gun was also removed.

Type K4: *RO.26-28* (ex-*Nos. 45, 58, 62*)

The design of this class was based on the earlier K3 Type, which had all been withdrawn from active service in April 1936. By 1939 this class was also obsolete and the vessels were withdrawn from active service in April 1940.

Type L4: *RO.60-68* (ex-*Nos.59, 72, 73, 84*)

This was a new design for an oceangoing submarine prepared in 1920. The class retained the same dimensions as the L3 Type, but internal improvements led to an increase in displacement. The 3-inch gun was resited on the fore-deck casing and an extra two torpedo tubes fitted in the bows. They were handy boats and the last to be based on British experience.

RO.58 c.1922. *Author's Collection*

RO.64. Author's Collection

Type KT: *RO.29-32* (ex-*Nos.68-71*)

This was a purely Japanese design prepared under the 1922-28 Law. It was based on experience gained from the Type K4 and an earlier K1 design (scrapped in 1932.). The vessels were powered by lighter diesels of a lower horsepower which led to a reduction in displacement. Being obsolete by 1939 these submarines were mainly used for training during the war.

RO.30. *Courtesy U.S. Navy*

I.152, June 18, 1939. *Author's Collection*

Type KD2: *I.52* (ex-*No.51*); renumbered *I.152* 5/42 KD3A*: *I.53-155, I.58* (ex-Nos.*64, 77, 78*); renumbered *I.153-155, I.158* 5/42 KD3B†: *I.56-57, I.59-60, I.63* (renumbered *I.156-157, I.159,* 5/42 KD4‡: *I.61-62* (ex-*No.64*); *I.62* renumbered *I.162* 5/42 KD5§: *I.65-67; I.65-66* renumbered *I.165-167* 5/42

These designs differed from the earlier KD1, being based upon the German *U.125* given to Japan as reparation at the end of World War I . Dimensions in the KD2 were increased but bunkerage was reduced, restricting the radius of action. Offensive capability was also curtailed by removing eight of the reload torpedoes. In this way displacement was kept down to that of the KD1 Type. The KD 3 Type differed slightly from the KD2 in having a redesigned conning tower. The KD5 Type carried a 3.9-inch high angle gun in place of the 4.7-inch carried in the earlier KD series. Ealy in 1945 *I.156-159* and *I.165* had the gun removed and chocks fitted to enable them to carry two Kaiten midgets.

I.58, September 1931. Note the streamlining effect at the front of the conning tower compared with *I.152. Author's Collection*

I.65, 1932. The Type KD5 vessels carried a 3.9in gun instead of the 4.7in of the earlier KD Type submarines. *I.W.M.*

Type J1: *I.1-4* (ex-*Nos.74-76*)

This was a long-range cruiser design based upon *U.125*. The conning tower was protected with light armour and sufficient stores were carried to enable the vessels to remain at sea unsupported for 60 days. When the supply situation on Japanese held Pacific Islands deteriorated towards the end of 1942, *I.1-2* were converted to transport submarines, the after gun being removed. A number of chocks were fitted to the deck casing aft of the conning tower on which a number of amphibious tanks or small 46-foot landing craft could be carried.

Type KRS: *I.21-24* (ex-*Nos.48-50*); renumbered *I.121-124* 5/42

This was the one and only class of minelaying submarine built by the Japanese and like the previous designs was based upon the German *U.125*. The mines were laid from vertical tubes in a special minelaying compartment aft. During 1940 these submarines were modified as supply submarines; petrol tanks were fitted to the deck casing and the submarines were to be stationed deep in enemy-held waters to refuel seaplanes. During August 1943 *I.121-122* were relegated to training.

I.1. *Author's Collection*

I.2. *Author's Collection*

I.22. *Author's Collection*

I.22 with a Kawanishi H6K (Emily) flying boat. *Author's Collection*

I.176, July 31, 1942. *I.W.M.*

Type KD6A: *I.68-73;* renumbered *I.168-169, 171-172* 5/42 KD6B*: *I.74-75*; renumbered *I.174-175* 5/42 KD7†: *I.76-85* + 10 units projected; renumbered *I.176-185* 5/42

This design was developed from the earlier KD series, dimensions being increased to permit the fitting of larger diesels. Towards the end of 1942 and early in 1943 *I.171, I.74, 176, 177* and *181* had the 4.7-inch gun and a number of reload torpedoes removed to enable them to act as transport submarines carrying a small landing craft.

I.5 on trials July 31, 1932. *Author's Collection*

Type J1M: *I.5* J2*: *I.6*

These were a modified J1 design. In order to improve the scouting capabilities of their submarines the Japanese decided to experiment with the carriage of small seaplanes. In order not to encumber the submarine with a large hangar (as in the British *M.2*) it was planned to house the main components of the seaplane in two large cylinders to port and starboard aft of the conning tower. It was found, however, that assembly of the aircraft took too long for safety and the equipment was removed during 1940.

The J2 Type was almost identical to the J1M but was fitted with more powerful diesels. *I.6* was originally to have mounted a 5-inch gun fore and aft of the conning tower, but to allow space for assembly of the seaplane it was decided to drop the after gun. *I.6* was fitted with a catapult for launching the seaplane aft of the conning tower.

I.8 arriving at Brest on August 14, 1943. Note the two raised housings to port and starboard abaft the conning tower. The seaplane was stored in sections in these two housings which retracted into the deck casing. *Author's Collection*

Type K5: *RO.33-34*

These two submarines were prototypes planned to gain experience with a standard design suitable for rapid production in the event of war. Greatly improved diesels were fitted and the 4.7-inch gun dropped in favour of the lighter 3-inch weapon.

Type J3: *I.7-8*

These submarines embodied experience gained with the operation of *I.5*. They were much larger and were equipped to act as flotilla leaders controlling the operations of a number of submarines at sea in areas far from the control of land headquarters. Seaplane arrangements remained the same as before with the addition of a catapult aft. *I.8* had the seaplane and 5.5-inch gun removed towards the end of 1944 to enable her to carry four Kaiten midgets.

Type A midget beached on Oahu Island after the raid on Pearl Harbour on December 12, 1941. *Courtesy U.S. Navy*

Type A: *Nos.1-2, Ha.1-52, 54-61*; B*: *Ha.53*; C*: Ha62-76

Initial experiments in the use of midget submarines began in the middle 1930's. These small craft were designed to carry out attacks on enemy bases. The Type A were powered solely by an electric motor which severely restricted their operational capabilities. This was overcome in subsequent models, which were powered by diesel/electric motors. The Type C midgets were designed for launching from specially adapted surface vessels.

No.71

This was an experimental submarine designed to test hull forms for small submarines with high underwater speed. Surface mobility was considered to be of secondary importance to submerged performance in this submarine and she was difficult to control on the surface. Exhaustive tests carried out with *No.71* led to the design of the Type ST and SS submarines.

Type C midget (*Ha.69*) being launched from Transport No. 5 on August 17, 1944. *Author's Collection*

I.15, September 15, 1940. *I.W.M.*

Type A1: *I.9-11*, Hull Nos. 700-701 A2*: *I.12* AM†: *I.1, I.13-15*, Hull Nos. 5094-5096

The design of these submarines was based upon experience gained with the J1M and J2 Types. The Type A1 were specifically fitted to co-ordinate the operations of 'Wolf-Pack' type attacks on enemy fleet units. Endurance was increased to 90 days and more powerful diesels fitted. The seaplane was housed in a large hangar which formed a forward extension of the conning tower while a catapult extended up to the bows.

The Type A2 were underpowered as diesel production was by then being allocated to A/S escorts. Extra bunkerage, however, increased the radius of action of the Type A2. The Type AM developed from the A2 was designed as a scouting submarine to replace the light cruisers of the Combined Fleet usually employed on this duty. The size of the hangar was increased to house two aircraft and it was offset to starboard under the conning tower. A primitive form of Schnorchel was fitted to the Type AM and became standard on all subsequent types of submarine.

Type B1: *I.15, 17, 19, 21, 23, 25-39* B2*: *I.40-45*, Hull Nos. 702-709 B3†: *I.54, 56, 58, 62-66*, Hull Nos. 5101-5114 B4‡: Hull Nos. 5115-5132 Projected

These designs were prepared in parallel with the Type A submarines and were designed to act as scouts for the attack groups controlled by the Type A. During the war a number of units had the hangar and catapult removed and a 5.5-inch gun mounted in front of the conning tower. Thus armed the vessels were used as attack submarines. Late in 1944 *I.36, 37, 44, 56* and *58* were modified to carry four Kaiten, the 5.5-inch gun, hangar and catapult being removed. *I.36, 56* and *58* were further modified early in 1945 to carry six Kaiten.

Conning tower of *I.36*. *Author's Collection*

Special landing barges equipped with caterpiller tracks aboard *I.15*. *Author's Collection*

I.54, 1944. Note catapult extending along foredeck casing, radar aerial on extension in front of the conning tower and main gun aft. *I.W.M.*

Type C1: *I.16, 18, 20, 22, 24* C2*: *I.46-51*, Hull Nos. 710-713 C3†: *I.52-53, 55, 57, 59*, Hull Nos. 5141-5155 C4‡: Hull Nos. 5156-5180 Projected

These attack submarines formed the third element of the pack groups comprising the Type A, B, and C submarines devised by the Japanese for ocean warfare. They were almost identical to the Type B except that they lacked the seaplane and carried instead two extra torpedo tubes. They were also equipped to carry a Type A midget submarine. Towards the end of 1942 *I.16* was modified for use as a transport submarine. *I.47, 48* and *53* were modified to carry four Kaiten at the end of 1944, *I.47* and *53* being subsequently equipped to carry six Kaiten.

I.16, March 9, 1940. *I.W.M.*

Type K6: *RO.35-56*, Hull Nos. 200-227 and 715-723

With war imminent the Japanese embarked on a large programme of oceangoing submarines. The K6 Type drew heavily on the experience gained with the prototype K5; tonnage, dimensions and bunkerage were increased and more powerful diesels fitted. Offensive capability was greatly improved with the introduction of the Type 95 torpedo. Of all the various designs produced by the Japanese these were probably the most successful.

RO.46, February 1944. *I.W.M.*

Type KS: *RO.100-117*, 9 units projected

These seagoing submarines were designed for operations around Japanese-held islands in the Pacific and were a lot smaller than the Type K6.

RO.109. Author's Collection

Type D1: *I.361-372*, 92 units projected D2*: *I.373-378*, 140 units projected

The difficulty of supplying Japanese-held islands in the Pacific led to the design of these transport submarines. Two 21-inch torpedo tubes were provided for in the original design but were dropped from production models. Following trials of *I.361* the bow section was lengthened and reshaped and the design of the conning tower modified to improve the seagoing performance. *I.361, 363, 366-370* and *372* were modified at the beginning of 1945 to carry five Kaiten, the 5.5-inch gun being removed.

Type SH: *I.351-353*, Hull Nos. 730-732

These submarines were designed as mobile supply bases for seaplanes, carrying 365 tons of aviation fuel, 11 tons of fresh water and a large store of bombs and torpedoes. The class was designed to carry a 5.5-inch gun but this was not fitted to production models.

Type STo: *I.400-417*, Hull No. 714

This design was produced to combine the roles of the Type A, B and C classes. It was planned that submarines of this class should carry out attacks on the Panama Canal and American west coast cities. The hangar was similar to that in the Type AM, but much larger. *I.402* was completed as a fuel tanker.

From left to right: *I.400, I.401, I.14. Courtesy U.S. Navy*

I.402 surrendered in September 1945. *Courtesy U.S. Navy*

Kairyu Suicide Type

During 1943 the Japanese produced a design for a suicide submarine based on the Type A midget. These vessels were slightly smaller than the midgets. Production commenced in February 1945 but delays and shortages led to numerous differences between units and bottlenecks in production. By the end of the war 215 had been completed while a further 207 were still under construction.

Type D Koryu.

Work on the design for a new midget submarine began in 1943, with size increased to allow a more powerful diesel to be fitted. The Koryu were designed to be mass produced but shortage of materials and heavy air raids severely curtailed the programme. By the end of the war only 115 had been completed, while a further 496 were still under construction.

Kaiten one-man suicide submarines. *Author's Collection*

Kairyu suicide submarines completing at Yokosuka Navy Yard in September 1945. *Courtesy U.S. Navy*

Type ST: *I.201-223*, 76 units projected

This design was developed from the experimental *No.71* (see above). They were mass produced in fully welded sections and were streamlined to improve submerged performance. The length-to-beam ratio was better than the German Type XXI to which they were similar, and they achieved a higher underwater speed. The 25mm guns were carried in retractable mounts.

Kaiten Suicide Type

This suicide weapon was designed in the Spring of 1944 and was developed from the body of a standard torpedo. Shortages of motors and other production difficulties led to many variations in design. By the end of the war 419 of these craft had been built.

Ha.202, February 1945. *Author's Collection.*

Type SS: *Ha.101-200*

These were small transport submarines designed for mass production. The design was simple and full electric welding was used in their construction. Exchanges of technical information with Germany led to the hulls of this class being coated with a rubber substance in an effort to foil radar and Sonar detection.

Type STS: *Ha.201-279, Ha.280-290* Projected

This design was a diminutive version of the Type ST based upon the experimental *No.71*. They were developed for coastal defence and were highly manoeuvrable. Equipment was kept to a minimum (as in the German Type XXIII, which they closely resembled) and the hulls were fully welded to speed production.

FOREIGN SUBMARINES

Ex-German Type IXC: *RO.500* (ex-*U.511*)
Ex-German Type IXC_{40}: *RO.501* (ex-*U.1224*)
Ex-German Type IXD_2: *I.501* (ex-*U.181*), *I.502* (ex-*U.862*)
Ex-German Type XB: *I.505* (ex-*U.219*)
Ex-German Type IXD_1: *I.506* (ex-*U.195*)
Ex-Italian Cappellini Class: *I.503* (ex-*UIT.24*, ex-COMMANDANTE CAPPELLINI)
Ex-Italian *Marconi* Class: *I.504* (ex-*UIT.25*, ex-LUIGI TORELLI)

CLASS	*71*	*A,B,C*	*KORYU*	*KAIRYU*	*KAITEN 1, 2*, 3†, 4‡*
TYPE	Experimental	Midget	Midget	Suicide	Suicide
DISPLACEMENT	195/240	/46(49¾*)	/59¾	/19¼	/18⅓(18½*, 18‡)
DIMENSIONS					
METRIC	42.8×3.3×3.1	23.9(24.9*)×1.8(2.5*)	26.2×2×2.8	17.3×1.4	48½(54*†‡)×3¼(4½*†‡)
IMPERIAL	140×10¾×10⅓	78½(81¾*)×6(8½*)	86×6¾×9½	56¾×4½	14.7(16.5*†‡)×1(1.37*†‡)
MACHINERY					
HP	1,200/1,800	600(40/600*)	150/500	85/80	550(1,500*‡1,800†)
SPEED	18/25	23(6½*)/19(18½*)	8/16	7½/10	30(40*‡)
RADIUS	3,830/33	300*/80(120*)	1,000/125	450/36	14¼(31*,23½†‡)
SPEED	12/7	6*/6(4*)	8/	5/3	30
FUEL					
DIVING LIMIT				80	
ARMAMENT					
GUNS	—	—	—	—	—
TORPEDO TUBES	3×457(18)	2×457(18)	2×457(18)	2×457(18)	—
SITING	3 bow	2 bow	2 bow	2 Underslung	—
NO OF TORPEDOES/	3	2	2	2 or 600Kg bow charge	1,550Kg warhead
MINES					
COMPLEMENT	80	2(3*)	5	2	1(2*†‡)

CLASS	*STS*	*K4*	*KT*	*KS*
TYPE	Coastal	Seagoing	Seagoing	Seagoing
DISPLACEMENT	320/493	746/1,070	665/1,000	525/782
DIMENSIONS				
METRIC	53×4×3.4	74.2×6.1×3.7	74.2×6.1×3.7	60.9×6×3.5
IMPERIAL	173¾×13×11¼	243×20×12¼	243×20×12½	200×19½×11½
MACHINERY				
HP	400/1,250	2,600/1,200	1,200/1,200	1,000/760
SPEED	10½/13	16/8	13/8	14½/8
RADIUS	3,000/100	6,000/85	6,000/85	3,500/60
SPEED	10/2	10/4	10/4	12/3
FUEL			60	
DIVING LIMIT	55		25	41
ARMAMENT				
GUNS	1×7.7	1×76(3)	1×120(4.7)	1×76(3)HA
TORPEDO TUBES	2×533(21)	1mg	1mg	
SITING	2 bow	4×533(21)	4×533(21)	4×533(21)
NO OF TORPEDOES/	4	4 bow	4 bow	4 bow
MINES		8	8	8
COMPLEMENT	22	45	43	38

CLASS	*L1, 2, 3*	*L4*	*K5*	*K6*	*ST*
TYPE	Oceangoing	Oceangoing	Oceangoing	Oceangoing	Oceangoing
DISPLACEMENT	893(889†)/1,195	988/1,322	700/1,200	960/1,447	1,070/1,450
DIMENSIONS					
METRIC	70.6(76.1†)×7.1×3.9	76.2×7.3×3.7	73×6.7×3.2	80.5×7×4	79×5.8×5.4
IMPERIAL	231½(250†)×23½×12¾	250×24½×12	239½×22×10½	264×23×13½	259×19×18

CLASS	*L1,2,3*	*L4*	*K5*	*K6*	*ST*
MACHINERY					
HP	2,400/1,600	2,400/1,600	3,000/1,200	4,200/1,200	2,750/5,000
SPEED	17/8	16/8	19/8¼	19¾/8	15¾/19
RADIUS	5,500/80	5,500/80	8,000/90	11,000/45	5,800/135
SPEED	10/4	10/4	12/3½	12/5	14/3
FUEL	65	75	100		
DIVING LIMIT	33		41	44	55
ARMAMENT					
GUNS	1×(3)HA 1mg	1×76(3) 1mg	1×76(3)HA 1×13	1×76(3)HA 2×25	2×25
TORPEDO TUBES	6(4*)×457(18) (4×533(21) in †)	6×533(21)	4×533(21)	4×533(21)	4×533(21)
SITING	4 bow (+2 broadside in *)	6 bow	4 bow	4 bow	4 bow
NO OF TORPEDOES/ MINES	10	10	10	10	10
COMPLEMENT	40(48†)	48	62	62	31

CLASS	*J1*	*J1M, J2*	*J3*	*A*
TYPE	Cruiser	Cruiser	Cruiser	Cruiser
DISPLACEMENT	1,970/2,791	2,080(,1900*)/2,921(3,061*)	2,231/3,583	2,434(2,390*,2,620†)/4,149(4,172*,4,762†)
DIMENSIONS				
METRIC	97.5×9.2×5	97.5(98.5*)×9.2(9*)×5(5.3*)	109.3×9×5.2	113.7×9.5(11.7†)×5.3(5.9†)
IMPERIAL	320×30¼×16½	320(323*)×30¼(29¾*)× 16½(17½*)	358½×29¾×17¼	372¾×31⅓(38½†)×17½(19⅓†)
MACHINERY				
HP	6,000/2,600	6,000(8,000*)/2,600	11,200/2,800	12,600(4,700*,4,400†)/2,400(1,200*,600†)
SPEED	18/8	18(20*)/7(7½*)	23/8	23½(17½*,16¾†)/8(6¼*,5½†)
RADIUS	24,400/60	24,000(20,000*)/60	14,000/60	16,000(22,000*,21,000†)/90(75*,60†,60†)
SPEED	10/3	10/3	16/3	16/3
FUEL				
DIVING LIMIT	44	44	55	55
ARMAMENT				
GUNS	2×140(5.5)	2×140(5.5)(1×127(5)HA in *) 1×13(in * only)	2×140(5.5) 5×13(2×1, 1×1)	1×140(5.5) 4(7†)×25(2×2)(2×3,1×1 in †)
TORPEDO TUBES	6×533(21)	6×533(21)	6×533(21)	6×533(21)
SITING	4 bow 2 stern	4 bow 2 stern	4 bow 2 stern	4 bow 2 stern
NO OF TORPEDOES/ MINES	20	20(17*) 1 seaplane	20, 1 seaplane	18(12†), 1(2†) seaplanes
COMPLEMENT	68	68	80	100(108†)

CLASS	*B*	*C*	*STO*
TYPE	Cruiser	Cruiser	Cruiser
DISPLACEMENT	2,198(2,320*,2,140†,2,800‡)/3,654(3,700*,3,688†)	2,184(2,095†,2,756‡)/3,561(3,700*,3,644†)	3,530/6,560
DIMENSIONS			
METRIC	108.7×9.3×5.1(5.2*†‡)	109.3(108.7†)×9.1(9*,9.3†)×5.3(5.1†)	122×12×7
IMPERIAL	356½×30½×16¾(17*†‡)	358½(356½†)×30(29¾*,30½†)× 17½(16¾†)	400×39×23
MACHINERY			
HP	12,600(11,000*,4,700†)/2,400(2,000*,1,200†)	12,600(12,400*,4,700†)/2,000(1,200†)	7,700/2,400
SPEED	23½(17¾†)/8(6½†)	23½(17¾†)/8(6½†)	18¾/6½
RADIUS	16,000(14,000*,21,000†)/90(96*,105†)	14,000(21,000†)/60(105†)	30,000/60
SPEED	16/3	16/3	16/3
FUEL			

DIVING LIMIT	55	55	55
ARMAMENT			
GUNS	1×140(5.5) 4(2*†)×25(2×2 or 1×2)	1(2†)×140(5.5) 2×25(2×1)	1×140(5.5) 10×25(3×3, 1×1)
TORPEDO TUBES	6×533(21)	8(6†)×533(21)	8×533(21)
SITING	4 bow 2 stern	4 bow 4 stern	4 bow 4 stern
NO OF TORPEDOES/ MINES	18(17*,19†) + 1 seaplane	20(19†)	20 + 3 seaplanes
COMPLEMENT	100(94*†)	95	144

CLASS	*KD1*	*KD2, 3, 4, 5*	*KD6, 7*
TYPE	Fleet	Fleet	Fleet
DISPLACEMENT	1,390/2,430	1,390(1,635*†‡,1,575§)/2,500(2,300*†‡,2,330§)	1,400(1,420*,1,630†)/ 2,440(2,564*,2,602†)
DIMENSIONS			
METRIC	91.4×8.8×4.5	100.8(100*,101†,97.5‡§)×7.6(8*†,7.8‡,8.2§)× 5.1(4.8*‡,4.9†,4.7§)	104.7(105*,105.5†)×8.2×4.5
IMPERIAL	300×29×15	330¾(330*,331†,320½‡§)×25(26*†,25½‡,26¾§) ×16¾(15¾*‡,16†,15½§)	343½(344½*,346†)×27×15
MACHINERY			
HP	5,200/2,000	6,800(6,000‡§)/2,000(1,800*†‡§)	9,000(8,000†)/1,800
SPEED	20/10	22(20*†‡,20½§)/10(8*†,8½‡,8¼§)	23/8¼(8†)
RADIUS	20,000/100	10,000/100(90*†,60‡§)	14,000(10,000*,8,000†)/65(50†)
SPEED	10/4	10/4(3*†‡§)	10(16*†)/3(5†)
FUEL		100	350*
DIVING LIMIT		32(41§)	41(38*42†).
ARMAMENT			
GUNS	1×120(4.7) 1×76(3)	1×120(4.7) (100 (3.9) in §) 1×13 (in § only)	1×100(3.9)HA (120 (4.7) in *† and I.171-173) 1(2*)13 (2×25 in †)
TORPEDO TUBES	8×533(21)	8(6 in ‡§)×533(21)	6×533(21)
SITING	6 bow 2 stern	6 bow 2 stern (6 bow only in ‡§)	4 bow 2 stern
NO OF TORPEDOES/ MINES	24	16(14 in ‡§)	14(12†)
COMPLEMENT	60	60	61(86†)

CLASS	*KRS*	*D*	*SH*	*SS*
TYPE	Minelaying	Transport	Supply Transport	Transport
DISPLACEMENT	1,142/1,768	1,440(1,660*)/2,215(2,240*)	2,650/4,290	370/493
DIMENSIONS				
METRIC	85.2×7.5×4.4	75.5(74*)×8.9×4.7(5§)	111×10.2×6	44.5×6.1×4
IMPERIAL	279½×24½×14½	248(242¾*)×29¼×15½(16½*)	363¾×33½×20	146×20×13¼
MACHINERY				
HP	2,400/1,100	1,850(1,750*)/1,200	3,700/1,200	400/150
SPEED	14½/7	13/6½	15¾/6⅓	10/5
RADIUS	10,500/40	15,000(5,000*)/120(100*)	13,000/100	3,000/46
SPEED	8/4½	10(13*)/3	14/3	10/2
FUEL				
DIVING LIMIT		41	50	55
ARMAMENT				
GUNS	1×140(5.5)	1×140(5.5) 2×25	4×76(3) mortar (2×2) 7×25 (2×2, 3×1)	1×25
TORPEDO TUBES	4×533(21)	—	4×533(21)	—
SITING	4 bow	—	4 bow	—

NO OF TORPEDOES MINES	12+42M	82 Tons cargo, (110*) 110 troops 2(1*)×14½ feet landing craft	4+390 Tons cargo + 60×250Kg bombs or 30×250Kg bombs + 15 aircraft torpedoes	60 Tons cargo
COMPLEMENT		60	77 + 13 aircrew	21

Name	Builder	In service	Fate
Ha.1-2	38	1936	
Ha.3-76	47		
Ha.101	35	11/44	Surr 8/45. Str.
Ha.102	35	11/44	Surr 8/45. Str
Ha.103	35	2/45	Surr 8/45. Sc 4/46
Ha.104	40	12/44	Surr 8/45. Str
Ha.105	35	2/45	Surr 8/45. Sc 4/46
Ha.106	40	12/44	Surr 8/45. Sc 4/46
Ha.107	40	2/45	Surr 8/45. Sc 4/46
Ha.108	35	5/45	Surr 8/45. Sc 4/46
Ha.109	40	3/45	Surr 8/45. Sc 4/46
Ha.110	35	—	Sc
Ha.111	40	7/45	Surr 8/45. Sc 4/46
Ha.112	40	—	Sc
Ha.113-200		—	Projected
Ha.201	49	5/45	Surr 8/45. Sc 4/46
Ha.202	49	5/45	Surr 8/45. Sc 4/46
Ha.203	49	6/45	Surr 8/45. Str 4/46
Ha.204	49	6/45	MC 10/45
Ha.205	49	7/45	Surr 8/45. Str 5/46
Ha.206	36	—	Surr 8/45. MC 25/8/45
Ha.207	49	8/45	Surr 8/45. Sc 4/46
Ha.208	49	8/45	Surr 8/45. Sc 4/46
Ha.209	49	8/45	Surr 8/45
Ha.210	49	8/45	Surr 8/45. Sc 4/46
Ha.211	36	—	Surr 8/45.Str 8/45
Ha.212	35	—	Surr 8/45. Str 6/46
Ha.213	40	—	Surr 8/45. Str 4/46
Ha.214	40	—	Surr 8/45. Str 4/46
Ha.215	49	—	Surr 8/45. Sc 4/46
Ha.216	49	8/45	Surr 8/45. Sc 4/46
Ha.217	49	—	Surr 8/45. Sc 4/46
Ha.218	49	—	Surr 8/45. MC 15/8/45
Ha.219	49	—	Surr 8/45. Sc 4/46
Ha.220	36	—	Surr & Sc 8/45
Ha.221	35	—	Surr 8/45. Str 6/46
Ha.222	36	—	Surr & Str 8/45
Ha.223	35	—	Surr & Str 8/45
Ha.224	40	—	Surr & Str 8/45
Ha.225	40	—	Surr & Str 8/45
Ha.226	40	—	Surr & Str 8/45
Ha.227	40	—	Surr & Str 8/45
Ha.228	49	—	Surr 8/45. Sc 4/46
Ha.229	49	—	Str & MC 8/45. CTL
Ha.230	49	—	Str & MC 8/45. CTL
Ha.231	49	—	Str & MC 8/45. CTL
Ha.232	49	—	Str & MC 8/45. CTL
Ha.233	36	—	Str & MC 8/45. CTL
Ha.234	35	—	Str & MC 8/45. CTL
Ha.235	36	—	Str & MC 8/45. CTL
Ha.236	35	—	Str & MC 8/45. CTL
Ha.237	40	—	Str & MC 8/45. CTL
Ha.238	40	—	Str & MC 8/45. CTL
Ha.239-240	40	—	Projected
H.241-245	49	—	Projected
Ha.246	36	—	MC 8/45. CTL
Ha.247	35	—	MC Str 8/45
Ha.248-249	35	—	Projected
Ha.250-253	40	—	Projected
Ha.254-258	49	—	Projected
Ha.259-262	35	—	Projected
Ha.263-266	40	—	Projected
Ha.267-271	49	—	Projected
Ha.272-275	35	—	Projected
Ha.276-279	40	—	Projected
Ha.280-290		—	Projected
I.1(1)	35	3/26	Lost 29/1/43
I.1(ii)	35	—	MC 25/8/45
I.2	35	7/26	Lost 7/4/44
I.3	35	11/26	Lost 10/12/42
I.4	35	12/29	Lost 20/12/42
I.5	35	10/32	Lost 19/7/44
I.6	35	5/35	Lost 30/6/44
I.7	38	3/37	Lost 22/6/43
I.8	35	10/38	Lost 31/3/45
I.9	38	2/41	Lost 13/6/43
I.10	35	10/41	Lost 4/7/44
I.11	35	5/42	MC 11/1/44
I.12	35	5/44	MC 5/1/45
I.13	35	12/44	Lost 15/7/45
I.14	35	3/45	Surr 8/45. Str 5/46
I.15(i)	38	9/40	Lost 2/11/42
I.15(ii)	35	—	Str 1946
I.16		3/40	Lost 19/5/44
I.17	60	1/41	Lost 19/8/43
I.18	49	1/41	Lost 11/2/43
I.19	40	4/41	Lost 18/10/43
I.20	40	9/40	MC 10/10/43
I.21	35	7/41	Lost 29/11/43
I.22	35	3/41	MC 1/10/42
I.23	60	9/41	MC 14/2/42
I.24	49	10/41	Lost 11/6/43
I.25	40	10/41	Lost 3/9/43
I.26	38	11/41	MC 25/10/44
I.27	49	2/42	Lost 12/2/44
I.28	40	2/42	Lost 17/5/42
I.29	60	2/42	Lost 26/7/44
I.30	38	2/42	Lost 13/10/42
I.31	60	5/42	Lost 12/5/43
I.32	49	4/42	Lost 24/3/44
I.33	40	6/42	MC 13/6/44
I.34	49	8/42	Lost 13/11/43
I.35	40	8/42	Lost 22/11/43
I.36	60	9/42	Surr 8/45. Sc 4/46
I.37	38	3/43	Lost 19/11/43
I.38	49	1/43	Lost 12/11/44
I.39	49	4/43	Lost 26/11/43
I.40	38	7/43	Lost 26/11/43
I.41	38	9/43	Lost 18/11/44
I.42	38	11/43	Lost 23/3/44
I.43	49	11/43	Lost 15/2/44
I.44	60	1/44	Lost 29/4/45
I.45	49	12/43	Lost 29/10/44
I.46	49	2/44	Lost 28/10/44
I.47	49	7/44	Surr 8/45. Sc 4/46
I.48	49	9/44	Lost 23/1/45
I.49-51(ii)			Canc 1943
I.51(i)	38	6/24	Str 4/40
I.52	38	12/43	Lost 24/6/44
I.53	38	2/44	Surr 8/45. Sc 4/46
I.54	60	3/44	Lost 25/10/44
I.55	38	4/44	Lost 28/7/44
I.56	60	6/44	Lost 18/4/45
I.57		—	Canc 1943
I.58	60	9/44	Surr 8/45. Sc 4/46
I.59		—	Canc 1943
I.60	49	12/29	Lost 17/1/42
I.61	40	4/29	MC 2/10/41. CTL
I.62		—	Canc 1943
I.63	49	12/28	MC 2/2/39. CTL
I.64(i)	38	8/30	Lost 17/5/42
I.64(ii)		—	Canc 1943
I.65		—	Canc 1943
I.66		—	Canc 1943
I.67	40	8/32	MC 29/8/40
I.70	49	11/35	Lost 10/12/41
I.73	35	1/37	Lost 26/1/42
I.121	35	3/27	Surr 8/45. Str 4/46
I.122	35	10/27	Lost 10/6/45
I.123	35	4/28	Lost 29/8/42
I.124	35	12/28	Lost 20/1/42
I.152	38	5/25	Str 8/42
I.153	38	3/27	Surr 8/45. Str 1946
I.154	49	12/27	Surr 8/45. Str 1946
I.155	38	9/27	Surr 8/45. Str 1946
I.156	38	3/29	Surr 8/45. Sc 4/46
I.157	38	12/29	Surr 8/45. Sc 4/46
I.158	60	5/28	Surr 8/45. Sc 4/46
I.159	60	3/30	Surr 8/45. Sc 4/46
I.162	40	3/30	Surr 8/45. Sc 4/46
I.165	38	12/32	Lost 27/6/45
I.166	49	11/32	Lost 17/7/44
I.168	38	7/34	Lost 27/7/43
I.169	40	9/35	Lost 4/4/44
I.171	35	12/35	Lost 1/2/44
I.172	40	1/37	Lost 11/11/42
I.174	35	8/38	MC 3/4/44
I.175	40	12/38	Lost 1/2/44
I.176	38	8/42	Lost 16/5/44
I.177	35	12/42	Lost 3/10/44
I.178	40	12/42	Lost 29/5/43
I.179	35	6/43	MC 14/7/43
I.180	60	1/43	Lost 27/4/44
I.181	38	5/43	Lost 16/1/44
I.182	60	5/43	Lost 1/9/43
I.183	35	10/43	Lost 28/4/44
I.184	60	10/43	Lost 19/6/44
I.185	60	9/43	Lost 22/6/44
I.201	38	2/45	Surr 8/45. Sc 11/45
I.202	38	2/45	Surr 8/45. Sc 4/46
I.203	38	5/45	Surr 8/45. Sc 11/45
I.204	38	—	Lost 22/6/45
I.205	38	—	Lost 28/7/45
I.206	38	—	Str
I.207	38	—	Str 1946
I.208	38	—	Str 1946
I.209-223		—	Canc 1945
I.351	38	1/45	Lost 14/7/45
I.352	38	—	Lost 22/6/45
I.353		—	Canc
I.361	38	5/44	Lost 30/5/45
I.362	40	5/44	Lost 18/1/45

Name	Builder	In service	Fate
I.363	38	7/44	Lost 29/10/45
I.364	40	6/44	Lost 16/9/44
I.365	60	8/44	Lost 28/11/44
I.366	40	8/44	Surr 8/45. Sc 4/46
I.367	40	8/44	Surr 8/45. Sc 4/46
I.368	60	8/44	Lost 27/2/45
I.369	60	10/44	Surr 8/45. Str
I.370	40	9/44	Lost 26/2/45
I.371	40	10/44	Lost 24/2/45
I.372	60	11/44	Lost 18/7/45
I.373	60	4/45	Lost 13/8/45
I.374	60	—	Str
I.375-378		—	Canc
I.400	38	12/44	Surr 8/45. Sc 6/46
I.401	49	1/45	Surr 8/45. Sc 6/46
I.402	49	7/45	Surr 8/45. Sc 4/46
I.403		—	Canc 1945
I.404	38	—	MC 28/7/45
I.405	36	—	Str
I.406-417		—	Canc 3/45
I.501	3	5/45	Surr 8/45. Sc 2/46
I.502	3	5/45	Surr 8/45. Sc 2/46
I.503	45	5/45	Surr 8/45. Sc 4/46
I.504	45	5/45	Surr 8/45. Sc 4/46
I.505	30	5/45	Surr 8/45. Str 1948
I.506	3	5/45	Surr 8/45. Str 1947
RO.26	49	1/23	Str 4/40
RO.27	60	7/24	Str 4/40
RO.28	49	11/23	Str 4/40
RO.29	35	9/23	Str 4/36
RO.30	35	1/24	Str 4/42
RO.31	35	5/27	Surr 8/45. Sc 4/46
RO.32	35	5/45	Surr 8/45
RO.33	38	10/35	Lost 29/8/42
RO.34	40	5/37	Lost 5/4/43
RO.35	40	3/43	Lost 25/8/43
RO.36	40	5/43	Lost 13/6/44
RO.37	40	6/43	Lost 22/1/44
RO.38	40	7/43	Lost 11/11/43
RO.39	49	9/43	Lost 2/2/44
RO.40	40	9/43	Lost 15/2/44
RO.41	40	11/43	Lost 23/3/45
RO.42	49	8/43	Lost 10/6/44
RO.43	40	12/43	Lost 26/2/45
RO.44	42	9/43	Lost 16/6/44
RO.45	40	1/44	Lost 30/4/44
RO.46	42	2/44	Lost 18/4/45
RO.47	40	1/44	Lost 26/9/44
RO.48	40	3/44	Lost 14/7/44
RO.49	42	5/44	Lost 4/4/45
RO.50	42	7/44	Surr 8/45. Sc 4/46
RO.50-54		—	Canc 1943
RO.55	42	9/44	Lost 7/2/45
RO.56	42	11/44	Lost 9/4/45
RO.60	40	9/23	Lost 29/12/41
RO.61	40	2/24	Lost 31/8/42
RO.62	40	7/24	Surr 8/45. Str 1946
RO.63	40	12/24	Surr 8/45. Str 1946
RO.64	40	4/25	Lost 12/4/45
RO.65	40	6/26	MC 3/11/42
RO.66	40	7/27	MC 12/12/41
RO.67	40	12/26	Surr 8/45. Str 7/46
RO.68	40	10/25	Surr 8/45. Str 4/46
RO.70-74		—	Canc 1943
RO.75			Renumbered *RO.56*
RO.76-99			Canc 1943
RO.100	38	9/42	Lost 25/11/43
RO.101	35	10/42	Lost 15/9/43
RO.102	35	11/42	Lost 14/5/43
RO.103	38	10/42	Lost 28/7/43
RO.104	35	2/43	Lost 23/5/44
RO.105	35	3/43	Lost 31/5/44
RO.106	38	12/42	Lost 22/5/44
RO.107	38	12/42	Lost 12/7/43
RO.108	35	4/43	Lost 26/5/44
RO.109	35	4/43	Lost 25/4/45
RO.110	35	7/43	Lost 11/2/44
RO.111	35	7/43	Lost 11/6/44
RO.112	35	9/43	Lost 11/2/45
RO.113	35	10/43	Lost 12/2/45
RO.114	35	11/43	Lost 17/6/44
RO.115	35	11/43	Lost 31/1/45
RO.116	35	1/44	Lost 24/5/44
RO.117	35	1/44	Lost 17/6/44
RO.200-227		—	Canc 1943
RO.500	21	9/43	Surr 8/45. Str 4/46
RO.501	21	2/44	Lost 13/5/44
No.71	38	8/39	Str 1941

NOTE. A number of vessels listed as MC 8/45 sank during a typhoon on 25/8/45.

ROMANIA

Quarnaro design: DELFINFUL

Romania ordered her first submarine from Italy early in 1927. It was built to a fairly standard design for a seagoing submarine. The vessel was completed in 1931 but was not finally taken over by Romania until May 1936.

German design: MARSOUINUL

This submarine was built in Romania to a German design. The vessel was laid down in 1938 and completed in 1942. She was slightly smaller than the *Delfinul* but more powerful diesels gave her a better surfaced speed.

German Design: REQUINUL

Like the previous submarine this vessel was built in Romania to a German design. Dimensions remained much the same but displacement was reduced still further by the complete removal of all stern torpedo tubes. Part of the after section of the hull was designed for the carriage of mines, the basic design of the rest of the vessel being much the same as the *Marsouinul*.

FOREIGN SUBMARINES

Ex-Italian: *CB* Class: *CB1-4,6*

CLASS	*DELFINUL*	*MARSOUINUL*	*REQUINUL*
TYPE	Seagoing	Seagoing	Minelaying
DISPLACEMENT	650/900	620/	585
DIMENSIONS			
METRIC	68.6×5.9×3.6	58×5.6×3.6	65×5.9×3.6
IMPERIAL	225×19½×12	190×18½×11¾	.223×19½×12
MACHINERY			
HP		1,840/	1,840/
SPEED	14/9	16/9	17/9
RADIUS			
SPEED			
FUEL			
DIVING LIMIT			
ARMAMENT			
GUNS	1×102(4)	1×105(4.1) 1×37	—
TORPEDO TUBES	8×533(21)	6×533(21)	4×533(21)
SITING	4 bow, 4 stern	4 bow, 2 stern	4 bow
NO OF TORPEDOES/ MINES			+ 40M
COMPLEMENT			

Name	Builder	In Service	Fate
CBI-6	13	9/43	
Delfinul	11	5/36	Str 1957
Marsouinul	29	1942	Str 1967
Requinul	29	1942	Str 1967

THAILAND

Mitsubishi Type: BLAI JUMBOL, MACHANU, SINSAMUDR, VIRUN + 4 Projected

These four submarines were built in Japan to a private design of the Mitsubishi Company. This coastal design was an entirely new concept for the Mitsubishi yard as Japan had never shown great interest in coastal designs. All four vessels were laid down in 1936. It had been planned to build four more, but owing to the likelihood of war the orders were never placed.

CLASS	*BLAI JUMBOL*
TYPE	Coastal
DISPLACEMENT	374½/430
DIMENSIONS	
METRIC	51×4.1×3.6
IMPERIAL	167×13½×12
MACHINERY	
HP	1,100
SPEED	10/6
RADIUS	4,770
SPEED	
FUEL	
DIVING LIMIT	
ARMAMENT	
GUNS	1×76(3),1×25,1×8
TORPEDO TUBES	5×450(18)
SITING	4 bow, 1 stern
NO OF TORPEDOES/ MINES	
COMPLEMENT	33

Name	Builder	In Service	Fate
Blai Jumbol	65	1938	Str 1950
Machanu	65	1938	Str 1950
Sinsamudr	65	1938	Str 1950
Virun	65	1938	Str 1950

Majchanu. *Courtesy Royal Thai Navy*

GUNS

BORE[1]	CALIBRE	COUNTRY	MODEL[2]	MUZZLE VELOCITY[3]	WEIGHT OF PROJECTILE	ROUNDS PER MINUTE	RANGE[5]
140/5.5	40	JAPAN	1925	700/2,296½	38/83¾		16,000/17,500*
127/5	45	GERMANY	1934	885/2,700	27½/61¾		10,500/11,480*
127/5	40	JAPAN	1930	780/2,380	22½/50¾		14,700/16,200
120/4.7	45	ITALY	1931	730/2,220	22/49½	8	14,500/15,850
120/4.7	45	JAPAN	1927	825/2,706½	20/45		16,000/17,500
120/4.7	12	JAPAN	1941	312/950	12¾/28¾		5,300/5,800
105/4.1	45	GERMANY	1932	845/2,575	14¾/33⅓		10,000/10,940
105/4.1	65	GERMANY	1933	970/2,953	14¾/33⅓		10,250/11,260
102/4	35	ITALY		755/2,300	15/33¾	7	
100/3.9	47	ITALY	1931-8	840/2,560	13¾/31	8	12,600/13,800
100/3.9	50	JAPAN	1930	950/2,900	12¾/28¾		16,600/17,700
100/3.9	65	JAPAN	1940	1,085/3,300	12¾/28¾		19,300/21,320
88/3.5	45	GERMANY	1930	850/2,592	9½/21½		14,200/15,530
88/3.5	75	GERMANY	1932	1,020/3,117	9½/21½		17,100/18,700
76/3	23	JAPAN	1930	484/1,475	5¾/12¾		7,680/8,400
76/3	60	JAPAN	1941	968/2,950	6/13¼		13,500/14,750

NOTES

1. The diameter of the bore is quoted in millimetres/inches
2. Year of design
3. Metres/feet per second
4. Kilogrammes/pounds
5. Maximum (normally given for 45° elevation, or at 30° when marked thus*) Metres/yards.

TORPEDOES

BORE[1]	COUNTRY	MODEL[2]	WEIGHTS TOTAL	WEIGHTS EXPLOSIVE	PISTOL	PROPULSION[4]	RANGE[5]
533/21	GERMANY	/G7e		294/660	MAGNETIC	ELECTRIC	4,560/5,000@ 30
533/21	ITALY			250/560			3,000/3,280 @ 40 12,000/13,100 @ 26
533/21	ITALY			260/585			4,000/ 4,380 @ 43 12,000/13,150 @ 30
533/21	ITALY			270/608			4,000/4,380 @ 48
533/21	JAPAN	1940/92	2,640/5,940	294/660	CONTACT	ELECTRIC	7,000/7,660 @ 30
533/21	JAPAN	1942/96	1,625/3,660	396/891	CONTACT	OXYGEN/PARAFFIN	4,480/4,900 @ 48
450/17.7	ITALY	1913		110/248	CONTACT		2,000/2,190 @ 38
450/17.7	ITALY	1914		115/254	CONTACT		6,000/6,570 @ 26 2,000/2,190 @ 38
450/17.7	ITALY			200/450			3,000/3,280 @ 44
457/18	JAPAN	1942/98	890/2,000	342/770		OXYGEN/PARAFFIN	3,200/3,500 @ 41

NOTES

1. Diameter of torpedo in millimetres/inches
2. Year of design
3. Kilogrammes/pounds
4. Source of power
5. Metres/yards @ knots